PILTDOWNLAD NO.6

INSTITUTIONALIZED

The "Institutionalized" story cycle is an exploration of abuse from the perspectives of the abused and the abusers.

"A powerful, humanizing work."
-- Broken Pencil

"This powerful zine demonstrates what it means to create space... shape shifting and, at times, completely absurd."
-- Maximum Rocknroll

"You can't get much more real that this. A brave zine..."
-- Craven Rock

"...essential reading."
-- One Minute Zine Reviews

INTRO

So far, only a few people have noticed that Piltdownlad #7 came out before #6. This non-sequential publishing schedule is the result of my original plan to put out the "Institutionalized" story cycle after The Detour Guide (#5), which I semi-finalized by making an announcement in the back of that issue. Since then, however, various obstacles (read: life) have prevented me from making it happen. In the meantime, I released "The Murky Realm," a story about my parents and their unusual courtship, as Piltdownlad #7. This helped get the juices flowing again and I began work on #6 shortly after that. (see appx. 1) Now that I have rounded the corner with this latest issue, I've come to accept that, as much as I want to fill each issue of Piltdownlad with a variety of material, I can only use what comes out and not what I wish I could force out. So this time around, I've stuck to the one story (or cycle, as it were), but I've included letters and some commentary on the zines I've been reading lately. I'm not making any decisions on #8 yet. I'll see what happens after I get this one printed.

Okay, first, some explanation on what this "story cycle" bullshit is all about...

I started writing about the dysfunction and trauma in my family almost four years ago. My original intention, since I've always fancied myself a "literary" guy, was to write a novel in the tradition of Faulkner and Tolstoy, an epic portrait of my family written in the third person from all the different perspectives. Ambitious? Yes, I know. Arrogant? Completely. But I figured that if I failed, the end result would be closer to what I wanted to accomplish than if I started out on a smaller scale. This is a BIG story and extremely convoluted. To say the least.

The first draft was 850 pages. It was, unsurprisingly, a complete mess. An utter failure. I had tried to cram too much information into one story. A common rookie mistake. I had tried, in the past, to write a longer work, but always gave up before I made it past page 100. So, after licking my wounds, I rewrote it in the first person, from my perspective only this time, as a teenager experiencing the events as they happened. That is what became, after numerous rewrites and soul-wrenching edits, the novel I published earlier this year, A Masque of Infamy. (see appx. 2)

While most of the first draft was scrapped, there were a few parts that I really liked. I thought the part of the story when my little brother and I are initially taken into custody and put in a mental hospital while our father and Rick waited to be arrested on sodomy and child abuse charges was particularly poignant when told from all four perspectives. So I went back in, salvaged and rewrote these sections for this current version I've entitled, "Institutionalized." (see appx. 3)

As I was writing the first draft, to get at the grist of the story, I interviewed my siblings and my father several times. I obtained the court records from the trial and the newspaper articles from The Anniston Star. (see appx. 4) Some of these documents are printed herein.

A few additional notes: There is, as usual, some "creative engineering" to maintain the narrative and flesh out the characters through dialogue.

All names have been changed and/or redacted. Even my own.

This is consistent with the names in the novel and done to avoid any hassles with certain people (see appx 5) not liking what I've written about them. (see appx. 6) This way, I can just point out, Hey, it's FICTION! (see appx. 7) It's a novel! (see appx. 8) And anyway, I knew from the beginning that I didn't want to write a memoir and face all the flak memoirs usually get. (see appx. 9)

While changing names to protect the victims and innocent bystanders in this story would seem to make sense, why, you might be wondering, did I remove the names of the perpetrators? I went back and forth over that point, but decided that since they'd served their time, their debt to society was paid. What they may owe me, my brother and the rest of our family, is debatable at this point. It's been 25 years. (see appx. 10)

The "Institutionalized" story structure is preceded with an introduction cannibalized from Piltdownlad #4. (see appx. 11)

Okay, that's it.
Thanks for reading.

LETTERS & COMMENT

Write to PILTDOWNLAD **Po Box 22974**
Oakland, CA 94609

Hi Kelly,
Thanks so much for sending me a copy of your zine. I really enjoyed it. After doing numerous rounds of line edits on my newest issue, I can't tell you how impressed I am that you typed yours. I'm also impressed at how you've transcended your past. After working for the Youthcorps one year, I spent the winter working at a shelter for MR/DD girls (Mental retarded/developmentally disabled) and an institute for teenage sexual offenders. About 80% of the kids I worked with had suffered some sort of abuse within the foster care system. It was really depressing and I quickly realized I don't have the fortitude to work in such fucked-up environments, even though caring professionals are what the system needs.
    Lia   The People I Love Best

Hey Kelly,
Last week I picked up a couple of your zines from the Vancouver public library's zine section. Since you obviously enjoy receiving mail (and who doesn't?) I thought it appropriate to send you a note and a zine. I read Piltdownlad #2 and #5 and enjoyed reading them both cover to cover. Speaking of, nice cover stock. I've never fussed too much about my paper options (cheap works fine) but it's always something I notice in other zines (and appreciate more if subtle). Women Got Me Drinking was a fast and funny read--religious hobos and girl woes, and some great lessons from the landscape of work. Maybe I'm a bit sick, but I love reading about people working jobs that take them to interesting thoughts and actions. It was good to see another art-cart story in The Detour Guide. What a crazy time. You're an excellent storyteller. The lively, energetic illustrations are a nice complement to the orderly typewritten pages. The Pirate story is my favorite from this issue, though it's a tough choice.
    Rodney Dickinson

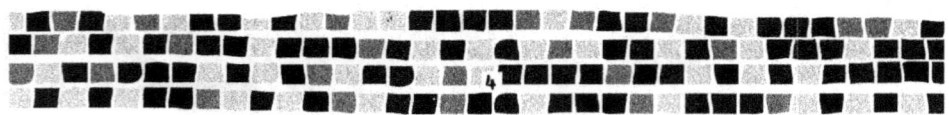

P-ISSED O-FF BOX

Kelly,

Hey, I saw your comment on Sage's blog (Sweet Candy Distro), as well as your review, and thought I'd drop you a line.

I see that you tried to mail me something and it came back. It's very strange. This particular postal box (I've had them all over the country, from coast to coast, for two decades) has given me the most trouble I've ever had. The ironic thing is that the mail I'm receiving in 2012 is probably the least weird mail that I've gotten in twenty years. On top of that, I'm using my real name, instead of an alias. But, a couple months ago, I caught the postal clerk starting to send something back that was addressed to me. I was picking up a package and he said, "Oh there was something else, but I didn't think it was for you." He brings up a standard half-size zine envelope without any weird drawings or whatever, and it was addressed to "Loran." He says, "That's not you, is it?" I tell him that yes, it's me, and he says, "Well, we better stick that name on your box, I guess." Now, here's the weird thing, that's my actual name. It's on every bill they stick in my box, it was on the package that he handed me that day, which was too large to fit but which didn't get sent back. It's the name on the credit card I use to pay my postal rent. It's on a dozen pieces of mail that somehow make it to my box every week. But, for whatever reason, the lack of a last name caused great chaos, I guess. On top of that, not a week goes by that I don't get mail from previous box owners. Why doesn't that mail get send back? It makes no sense. I came back the next day and tried to have a civil conversation about how long he'd been sending my mail back, and he said it was the first time. Now I know why I never really got more than two or three orders for that last zine. Hopefully, I've resolved everything at this point, but only time will tell. I've got no plans on getting rid of that box, so hopefully they'll get used to my crazy name.

Thanks for your kind review. Where did you run across my zine? I don't think that I recognize yours, so I'm guessing that we never traded. Were you one of my three orders from Xerography Debt and I'm just not remembering your name? If so, I'm sorry for that.

I've enclosed a copy of my latest, perhaps you can trade me a copy of yours with the review. That would be nice.

Loran

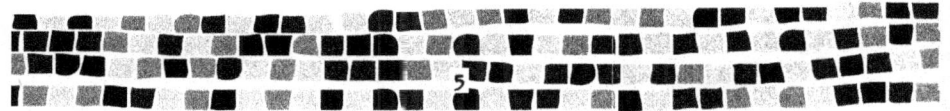

I reviewed Loran's zine **The Blurry Line** in issue #5.
I really liked that zine and was just as impressed with
his new one, **I Keep Interrupting Myself**. Loran spins
a story in such a tangential way that it's amazing that
he can still make it back to the original thread. It's
like listening to a drunk guy tell a crazy story that
involves all these characters and aspects that lead in
various directions, but just when you're about to get
lost in an alternate tale, he pulls you back into the
main narrative and you realize you might be drunker
than the guy telling the story. I **Keep Interrupting
Myself** is about sales tax tokens, but that's just the
starting and ending point. The fun parts are what he
adds along the way. $2 a copy. Write to Loran:
PO Box 2600, Sarasota, FL 34230. (New address.)

Hiya!
Hope all is well as can be. Been meaning to write
and say that I enjoyed the 5 issues of yr zine I
traded for at the PDX Symposium. Love personal
stories, but also how you feel about zines in
general. Felt a lot of commonality. Keep on writing
and catch you next time.
Ryan Mishap
PO Box 5841, Eugene, OR 97405

Hello Kelly,
Please forgive the tardiness of this response.
I'm still trying to answer all of the mail, but it
takes me a while!
Many thanks for the copy of Nasty Oh-Dear. I
enjoyed the read and very much appreciated the
Dischord shout-out.
Yours,
Ian

felt free to write the story I needed to tell. It doesn't release me from the responsibility of how my family reacts, but I am able to assuage some of my siblings concerns by changing names. My little brother, who features the most prominently in my story, has gone back and forth about it, alternately threatening to sue me and giving me his blessing. Which is a shame because I think I've done his suffering justice. He's only read a small amout of what I've written. He has a hard time dealing with the past and lives with more resentment and anger than a human being should, I think.

Billy accompanied his letter with his zine Proof I Exist, issue 12, which details his move from Chicago to New Mexico. I really enjoy his writing. It's forward and candid and fun. Billy seems like he'd be a blast to hang out with. (We connected at the Portland Zine Symposium, but it was a brief encounter.) Billy's got a keen perspective on the world around him and a lot to say about it and his place in it. In this issue, Billy decides one day to up and leave Chicago after ten years and head out west to New Mexico with only a few leads and the slight possibility of a friend there to help him out. He loads up a U-Haul and drives cross country with his dog. What's impressive about his experience, besides fulfilling the dream of anybody who ever felt stuck in one place, is that within a week (the time span covered in this zine), he manages to get situated with only a modicum of anxiety and just a little assistance (once he turned in the U-Haul, he didn't have transportation). I can't help but admire Billy's tenacity and verve. After finishing PIE #12, I started reading the other zine he sent me: A Night at The Casino. This zine is about his work as a craps dealer. Again, Billy has a strong voice and his stories of the other dealers, the gamblers and life inside a casino are informative and interesting. Billy's zines are top notch. I've also acquired his novel, Harold's Horrible Life, which I look forward to reading. I have to say, after trading zines for so long, it feels great to trade books. Email Billy: iknowbilly@gmail.com

---

Address all correspondence to the address on the last page. I'll write back. Sometimes I can be a little slow to respond, but I won't forget about you. And if you don't want your letter printed in future issues, please let me know. Remember, too, if you use an alias, be sure and sign off with it. I'm an old man. I get confused easily.

TALKING ABOUT TYPEWRITERS

Kelly,

Feel free to publish anything you wish from any of the letters I send you unless I request otherwise. Thanks for asking, but you don't need to do so in the future. I look forward to your letters and comments section.

Your type looks nice and crisp on the kind of paper you wrote your letter to me on. I suppose that's the same paper you use when composing the type copy for your zine. It looks like it does a lot to reduce the fuzzy edges of type produced with a fabric ribbon, especially if it's for publication. (I don't have that problem myself because I use carbon film ribbons, which look quite acceptable on regular old bond paper.)

This letter right here has been typed on one of my IBM Executive typewriters. (The typeface is called Modern.) The really useful thing about the IBM Exec is that it has proportional spacing --- letters are narrower or wider depending on their width in traditional type fonts. Notice that I've typed each   iiiii of the letters to the right   eeeee five times each, but the   wwwww lines get longer as the   mmmmm width increases. This makes the final type copy look more like real print. (Most typewriters have standard, or unit, spacing, where all letters are the same width.) Proportional spacing makes the final copy look really superb if you type each line twice in order to get right-justified columns, which you would do by typing a line once, tabbing over, and typing it again with space added or subtracted between words. I like right-justified columns because they look professional and they look like real print as you would see it in a newspaper or magazine. If you're interested, I could tell you more about these typewriters.

I have an Olympia, too, and the type from it looks just like yours. I found it at a thrift store. It's the finest manual typewriter I own. (The others are Royal Quiet deLuxes, and a couple of Smith-Coronas.) I think I have about five different typefaces among my manual typewriters, and it's about the same with my IBM Executives. Some of those are in pretty good condition, while others are pretty beat up from heavy use and/or shipping damage that occurred due to improper handling or packing.

We don't have Kelly Paper around here. It's X-Ped-X --- and they're so far out in the county (I don't have a car) that it's often easier for me to pick up a couple of reams at the FedEx office that's on the bus line, or stock up there on regular bond and pay the $10 cab fare to bring a couple of cases to my printing space. All my other supplies (ink, film, plates) come by mail order. Ribbons I buy second hand from EBay sellers.

I think it's a slower groove doing all this extra work, and that's good because it forces me into the nitty gritty and focusses my mind on what I want to say and how I want it to look. I do all my writing by either longhand or typewriter. (Sometimes I wish I knew stenography, though, for when my thoughts come faster than I can write them down!)

I look forward to your next issue.

Doug Harrison

Doug Harrison doesn't use a typewriter for **The Zine Explorers' Notebook**, but each issue is printed on a salvaged Multilith offset press from 1957 and typeset on a Varityper and a Varigraph. Based on the description, it's an arduous process. From the Editor's Note in the last issue: "I love this work, in my way, but I don't do it for my own benefit, or for the mere act of worshipping technological artifacts. Rather, it's the connection that all of this work will foster that excites me, connection between my readers and me, and among my readers with each other." I can't recommend **The Zine Explorers' Notebook** enough, for content, style and creed. Send trade or $3 for 2 issues to: PO Box 5291, Richmond, VA 23220.

I love discussing typewriters, but I'm always quick to point out that, as much as I like the aesthetics, I write on a manual for economy and rhythm. It's easy to clatter one's fingers across the keyboard of a computer, but banging out words letter by letter on a manual is hard work. I find that certain passages or descriptives aren't worth the effort. And as I type, a natural beat emerges from the hammering of the keys, so that, in the end, the prose is lean and has a cadence that, I hope, keeps the reader engaged. I see my Olympia as a machine, an instrument. (But that doesn't mean I don't want to hear about other folks' experiences or impressions regarding the use of typewriters.

And if you type me a letter on the half sheet, I will probably reprint it in a future issue.)

Writing on a manual typewriter is a lot like playing a musical instrument. There is a rhythm to banging on the keys, and misstrokes can be unforgiving. You can rely on white-out, or just start over, but once you pull the sheet from the roller, the performance is over. I think the sense of permanence and consequence gives typewrittem prose its unique quality.

Also, since I have worked in design for over a decade and produced numerous books and magazines, creating a zine without using a computer is a challenge that makes it worthwhile.

ON THE ART OF RUNNING

Hello Kelly,
Thanks for sending me your zines out of the blue. I'm not sure I ever really thanked you for that. It's nice knowing you're in peoples' thoughts.

I have really been enjoying my typewriter. My brother collects them and he had cleaned up one of his for my birthday. I love the sound of the keys and the way my thoughts change as I am typing. It's not like writing on the computer where I can add and move and delete words easily. I think it gives my voice a different quality. A little rougher around the edges. A little more raw.

When I have a new zine finished I will be sure to send it your way. And if you are up for snail mail correspondence, that would be even more lovely. I have been writing so many letters lately. It's a joy to make people's mailbox a little more fun, and a lot less depressing.

Take care,
Nichole (nichole@illvision.net)

The latest issue of Nichole's zine **Pieces** (#8), picks up where the last one (a completely visceral mind-fuck of a perzine), left off. This time, instead of going deeper into the rabbit hole, she's heading to the shrink's office. In the **intro she mentions** that she knows she's not alone in her struggle to come to terms with psychotherapy. The issue is subtitled, "on twelve years of running," which is a succint way of describing the experience of knowing something is wrong and trying to avoid the problem. I've grappled with being on psych meds since I was a teenager. In the pages that follow, I recount how, at age 15, while in a mental hospital, I was first put on pills. They made me feel strange and I tried to stop taking them,

making up all sorts of excuses like they made the skin
on my fingers peel off. (What that was all about I
have no idea, though the doctor suggested it was from
the air-conditoning.) But they just kept giving me
new pills. There seemed to be an endless supply of
pills with all of their own various side effects.
After a while, I surrendered to the inevitable. When
the Wheel of Pill Fortune stopped, I ended up on an
anti-depressant called Imipramine. 100mg a day until
I was twenty-one and decided to get off them cold
turkey. I was in school at the time so I waited until
a break in classes. I spent the following days and
nights in a blur, paralyzed with a debilitating
weight inside me, as if my blood had turned to lead.
I lay on my bed, naked, cold and sweating, hoping the
waves of despair would eventually subside. After a
month, they did. But I still felt strange, in fact,
I've never been the same person I was before the
drugs. Whether this personality shift was a result of
the pills or just my natural development that had been
concealed by the drugs, I'll never know. My transition
from teenager to young adult was shrouded by the use
of Imipramine. This experience was enough to convince
me that psych meds were not something I wanted to ever
deal with again. But over the years, I've gone through
some pretty major rough patches and felt like I had
no choice but to try again. Always a new pill.
Always another side effect. (The worst one was what
I called "The Shrink And Drip.") So I never lasted
long. I'd get my shit together and move on. I have
mixed feelings about shrinks at best. The last time I
went to one, I only talked to
the guy for five minutes before he diagnosed me with
borderline personality disorder and prescribed some
anti-psychotic meds called Risperdole. I took them
for a week, but they turned me into a zombie, so I
gave up and never went back. I mean, BPD? The guy
was a quack. Still, there was definitely something
wrong with me. I had migraines, three or more a week.
I took 800mg of Advil almost daily. I had neck pains,
back pains, it hurt to sleep on my side, there was
this mysterious sensation in my ankle, my ears itched
all the time, I had toothaches and my eyes burned...
 All of which made me complain bitterly nonstop.
 I wasn't much fun to be around and I took
most of my frustration out on my wife. I was often
angry and things had to go my way or else! I was
protecting my disease. My disorder ruled my life and
by association, my wife's life. It was bad. And it
was getting worse. Last October, I sold everything
I owned, all my records, my CDs, my books and

memorabilia. I bought a one-way train ticket to
New Orleans. Packed a bag. Even before
the train was out of the LA area I knew I'd made a
huge mistake. Halfway through Texas, I completely lost
my shit. By the time I got to New Orleans, I was out
of my mind. My train arrived on a Sunday night. By
Monday afternoon, I was in a shrink's office. As I
sat there telling him about my current situation, 41
years old, separated from my wife, in a town two-
thousand miles from home, a place I'd lived in during
my twenties but where I currently didn't know a soul,
the reality of what I'd done became more intense. Then
I went into my whole backstory, the abuse, the mental
hospital, the years in foster care, the depression,
the suicide attempts, the broken relationships, the
lack of friends, the everlasting sense of always
being out of place, of FEELING out of place, and
feeling lost and confused... In the midst of it all,
I burst into tears. I hadn't been able to contain my
emotions since west Texas, but unburdening myself was
the final crack in the levee. It all came out against
my will. I was almost afraid the shrink was going to
throw me out of his office. Or worse, misdiagnose me
like the last guy. But once I was done, he calmly
asked if I was ready to do what it would take to get
better. I knew what he meant. I said yes. He put me on
150mg of Wellbutrin, 2mg of Ativan and 100mg of Sero-
quel. The next day I started seeing a therapist. I
worked my ass off for the next two months. All I could
think about was getting back to LA. Back to my wife.
Back to my home. I knew I couldn't keep running.

"INSTITUTIONALIZED"

1. The Adolescent Ward
2. Shit on a Shingle
3. POW
4. Group
5. The Hanged Man
6. Mister Nice Guy
7. Reckoning
8. Feeling Blocks

taught his son at home. In a bookshelf in the shack Tuesday were a set of encyclopedias and books on chemistry, the Civil War and electronics.

"I would bet even money that my son would do better on a geography test than half of the graduating seniors at Rutland High School," he

McCarty bought the shack and small parcel of land in 1984, according to town records.

"We called him the hermit," Judy Aungst, co-owner of a country store, said Tuesday. "We assumed he lived alone. Every day he would buy one sandwich and I would heat it for him and he would sit on the

Aug. 12, 1987

Soldiers accused of raping youth

By JOHN RONNER
Star Staff Writer

A 56-year-old Army reserve sergeant at Fort McClellan has been indicted on a charges that he raped and sodomized a preteen male relative. Police also allege that the sergeant took a pornographic photo of the boy having sex with a male reservist private

That private, the sergeant's 19-year-old homosexual lover, has also been charged with raping and sodomizing the boy

Police said the victim has been hospitalized for psychiatric treatment

The suspects were identified by police as Sgt ▮▮▮▮▮, 56 and Pvt ▮▮▮▮▮, both of 5606 Saks Road. Both work out of an office at Fort McClellan

The two reservists were indicted last week by the August term of the Calhoun County Grand Jury. They face a maximum penalty of life imprisonment if convicted.

The pair was held in the Calhoun County Jail on Tuesday under separate $50,000 bonds, charged with first-degree sodomy and first-degree sexual abuse. The sergeant was additionally charged with possession of child pornography.

Officers alleged that the child has

been sexually abused since around age five, including being repeatedly photographed in a series of sex acts.

The sergeant, originally from California, came to the Anniston area in a transfer.

Weeks ago, while ▮▮▮ and ▮▮▮ were out of town on a military exercise, social workers became aware of a possible problem and soon alerted Anniston police.

On July 10, officers raided ▮▮▮'s residence in Saks. Police said they seized a large amount of homosexual pornography, including magazines, novels and videocassettes.

Also confiscated were sexually-oriented letters between ▮▮▮ and ▮▮▮. In one letter, police alleged, the 19-year-old mentioned the preteen victim in a sexual context

The two suspects will appear in court for arraignment Aug. 19, at which they are to enter pleas to the charges.

Angled whiskers

Whiskers don't grow vertically from a man's skin, but emerge at angles of from 30 to 60 degrees. Seen microscopically, many whiskers appear from valleys in the skin; others from the top of "mountains," according to Wilkinson Sword.

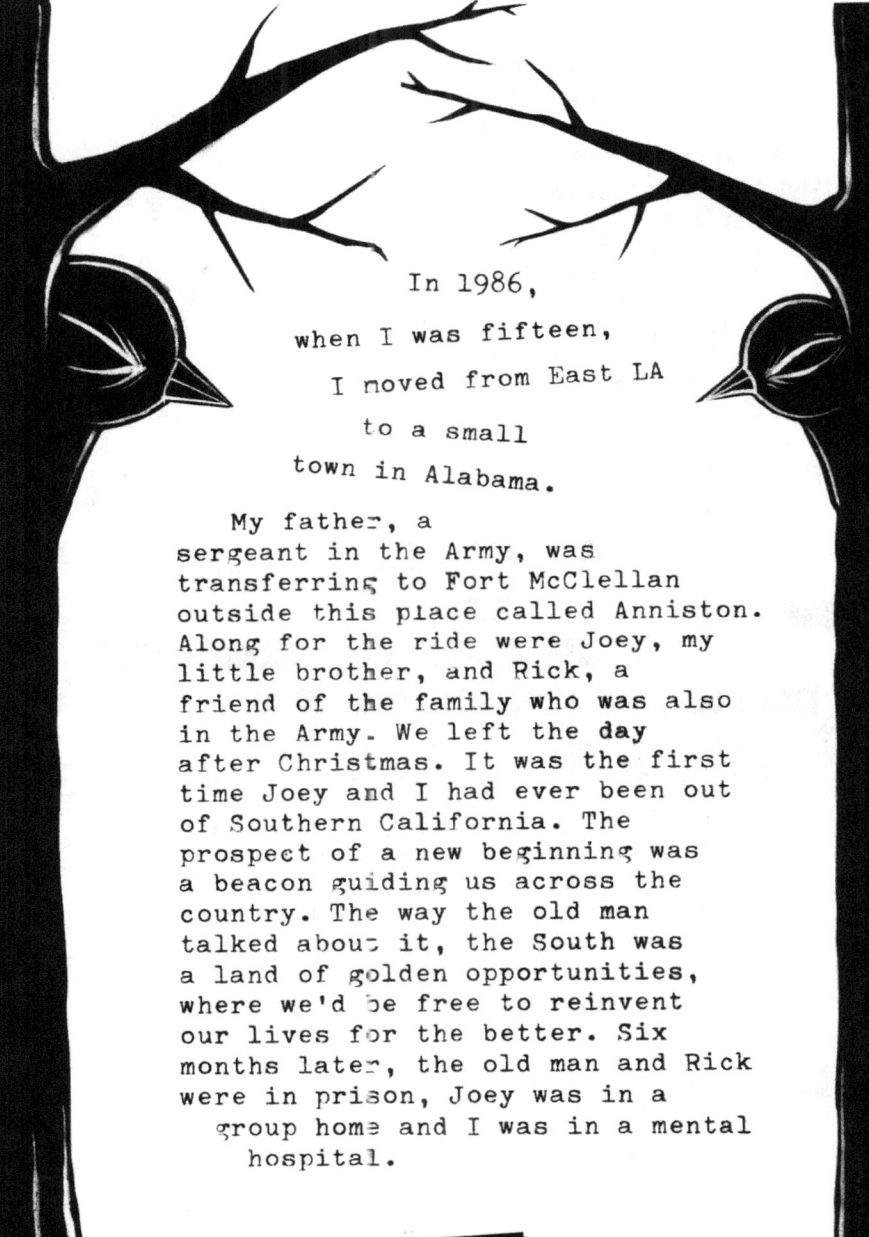

In 1986, when I was fifteen, I moved from East LA to a small town in Alabama.

My father, a sergeant in the Army, was transferring to Fort McClellan outside this place called Anniston. Along for the ride were Joey, my little brother, and Rick, a friend of the family who was also in the Army. We left the day after Christmas. It was the first time Joey and I had ever been out of Southern California. The prospect of a new beginning was a beacon guiding us across the country. The way the old man talked about it, the South was a land of golden opportunities, where we'd be free to reinvent our lives for the better. Six months later, the old man and Rick were in prison, Joey was in a group home and I was in a mental hospital.

For me, things were looking up.

For months the social workers had been pushing us to come clean about what was going on at the house. Of course, anybody who glanced at our situation twice knew things were fucked up. We were a total freakshow: four dudes from California living in a three bedroom house, with Rick and Joey sharing the master bedroom. There was the old man, so old he could've passed for our grandfather. There was Joey with his head shaved because Rick went in for the fresh recruit look. There was me, the raging punkrocker, constantly getting into trouble at school for making a scene with my outlandish wardrobe and FUCK YOU attitude. I didn't see why I had to tone down my style just because I was surrounded by a bunch of hillbillys.

And then there was Rick... Not only was he half-Japanese/half-Mexican and stood out like a sore thumb, but he was always out in the yard trying to get all buddy-buddy with the neighborhood boys like he'd done back home. Except what escaped attention in LA raised all sorts of flags in Anniston.

Until one day that summer when we were home alone for two weeks while the old man and Rick were off at some training camp in Georgia. Out of the blue, the ladies dropped by the house. They went into the same old routine, telling us, "You have nothing to lose. We know y'all must be scared, that's why we're here to protect you."

The social workers came snooping around a few months after we'd moved in, pulling Joey and me out of class and asking us fifty million questions. They were like Columbos on the case.

But Joey and I kept our mouths shut. "This is a rip-off," I couldn't deny Joey's claim

20

In the past, I'd always denied anything to the contrary, but this time I was desperate. Since I refused to get with the program and resisted Rick's authority like a feral beast, the old man was shipping me off to a boarding school in Mississippi.

A Christian boarding school.

It had all been set up. As soon as they got back from training camp, I was a goner.

When I pictured my life at that place, living in a dorm with rednecks, denied my music, my fashion, my cigarettes and having religion shoved down my throat every day, I just wanted to die. I thought about suicide all the time. How I could go into the woods behind the house with one of Rick's razor sharp buck knives, lean up against a tree and slash my wrists. I knew just how to get the job done right: lengthwise, to make sure the arteries were ripped open and I'd bleed out fast. Even though I was able to imagine myself lying there in the leaves and a pool of blood until somebody happened upon my corpse, I didn't have the guts to go through with it.

And then two days before the old man and Rick were due back, the social workers showed up and presented me with another option to escape my certain fate.

I told them to come back the next day and I might have something to show them. That night I talked to Joey. When I said that I'd found the polaroids he started to cry.

"Why are you crying? This is our way outa here."
"But I don't want anybody to think I'm... you know..."
"Fuck that! Rick's the fag. Which is why we're gonna make him pay. They'll buy us badass clothes and video games and all that shit. We'll get a free ride for sure."
"What about dad?"
"Fuck dad! We gotta look out for ourselves now."

It took some serious cajoling, but eventually Joey got on board. The next day, while the social workers sat at the kitchen table, I dropped the stack of polaroids, the letters, the magazines—everything I'd found in the old man's dresser when I was searching for cigarette money—right in front of them. Said, "Is that enough to get us outa here?"

As if I had to ask.
I could see the look on their faces.

That afternoon they drove us to the Jackson Home.

"Louis?"

Sometimes the way Joey said my name really grated my nerves. I knew he needed me. I'd gotten us into this mess and it was my job to get us out. But why couldn't he just be cool.

"Now what?"

The question had been gnawing at my guts as well: how the old man and Rick would react when they got home and saw what we'd done to the house. After we'd decided to give the polaroids to the social workers, we spent our last night at the house sitting around, worried about the next step in my master plan. But then I figured, why not go out with a bang. We broke into Rick's footlocker where he stored all his prized possessions, all the things we weren't allowed to touch. We hooked up the VCR and ate all the junk food. Once the sugar rush took hold, we grabbed Rick's pellet guns and started taking pot shots at the crap on his dresser. I made a couple bull's-eyes on the wall and we took turns practicing our aim. When we ran out of pellets, we switched to the knives. When the walls in his bedroom were full of holes, we moved on to the rest of the house. I stood at one end of the hallway and tried to see if I could hit the far wall. I missed, but I took out a lamp instead. Joey was an excellent shot. He had a good eye. He was the marksman, while I went for maximum destruction. We kept at it for several hours, from one room to the next. By the end of the night, the walls looked like they'd faced a firing squad. And we didn't stop there. We trashed everything in sight. We emptied the kitchen cupboards onto the floor. We smashed Rick's Nintendo into tiny fragments of plastic, wires and shards of motherboard. Before we went to sleep, I got a magic marker and scrawled "FEEL THE WRATH OF THE INNOCENTS" in giant letters on the living room wall.

No, there wasn't any doubt the old man and Rick would freak out when they saw that mess. But what about when they found out we'd told the social workers all their dirty secrets? That was a riddle I couldn't get my mind around. But with the nicotine withdrawals getting worse, I didn't want to talk about that bullshit.

Slowly, Joey struggled to find the words. "What do you think they're gonna do... when, uhm, they..."

"Fuck am I supposed to know? I snapped.

He didn't even need to say it.

I knew what he was getting at.

CC 87-1071

Assigned to Judge **Street**

Clerk's Form C-6 — SENTENCING JUDGE **Street**

CASE ACTION SUMMARY — CRIMINAL

Case Number CC— 87 1071

IN THE CIRCUIT COURT OF CALHOUN COUNTY — ☒ Fel

DEFENDANT: ~~[redacted]~~

OFFENSE (Charge):
I. Sodomy 13A-6-63
II. Sex. Abuse 13A-6-66
III. Poss. Obscene Matter 13A-12-192
IV. ~~[redacted]~~ 26-15-3

DEFENSE ATTORNEYS: **Bill Broome**

PROSECUTING ATTORNEY (for State): **Morgan**

Defendant's Address: 5606 Saks Rd.

STATE COURT I.D. No. (011015—Calhoun C.C.)

CASE NUMBER CC— 87 1071
DATE FILED (DOCKETED) O.C. 10-26-87
Grand Jury # 205 Date of Indict. 10-23-87
☐ Ret. ☐ App.
LOWER COURT NO.
☐ BLACK ☒ MALE
☒ WHITE ☐ FEMALE
D.O.B. 5-31-31
Occupation/Trade: **Clerk**
HEALTH __

COURT INFORMATION

CAPIAS — D.C. Warrant / Mun. Warrant / G.J-C.C. Writ
BOND — D.C. Bond / Mun. Bond / C.C. Bond — AMOUNT $10,000
INITIAL APPEARANCE — DATE
PRELIMINARY HEARING — ☐ Waived
DEFENDANT STATUS — Pers. Bond / Prof. Bond / Pers. Recog. — ☐ Co. Jail ☐ City Jail ☐ Prison
ARRESTING OFFICER — ☐ County ☐ State ☐ Conserv. ☐ Mun.

EXAMINER'S (AUDIT) NOTES

Date — Initials — Note

D.(S) **Plea Counts II & III** ACT ON FILINGS ORDERS 11/28/? MINUTES Bk. __ Pg. __

(Note: See file or other sheets for possible entries) (Judges initials)

Written "Not Guilty" Plea but Trial set: ___ 19 ___ M ( )

/-4-8? Arraigned. "Not Guilty" Plea. Trial set: ___ 19 ___ M ( )

11-24-8? See separate sheet for formal sentencing, etc.

11-5-87 Motion for Consolidation of Defendants - Order setting hearing 11-13-87 at 3:00 pm - copies to DA & Atty Broome

11-6-87 Motion to Compel Production and Disclosure

11-6-87 Order on Motion for Discovery Granted - Copies to Atty. Broome & DA

11-13-87 Deft present with Atty Bill Broome. Upon consideration of State's motion to consolidate, sue is hereby granted. (MRS)

— OVER —

THE ADOLESCENT WARD

One of the first things my new wardmates wanted to know about me was why I was there. It was an innocent enough question. One I would go on to ask all the admissions who arrived after me during the three months I was in the adolescent ward. Most volunteered the information freely, as if they were recounting what they'd seen on TV the night before. But on the day I showed up, I didn't know what to say. I'd forgotten to ask the social workers why they were taking my brother and me to a mental hospital.

Two weeks after dumping us in a shelter when they originally took us into custody, the ladies returned, all smiles and good cheer. Told us they were going to a new place in Birmingham called Hillcrest, where we'd be with kids our own age.

"It'll be like camp," Sandra said. "You'll have fun."

I looked at Joey. He cracked a smile for the first time since the last night at the house. This was what we'd been waiting for: our reward.

Birmingham!

The big city!

Before we hit the highway, the social workers made a few stops. First to their offices at the department of Human Resources where Clorise told us the old man and Rick had been arrested.

"They're being charged with sodomy, child abuse and possession of child pornography," she said nonchalantly. "If convicted, they could face up to life in prison."

I looked at Joey. "Life?"

They were giving me this information because I'd demanded to be a part of the process when I made the deal to turn my father in. But after I learned the old man's fate, I wished I'd never asked to be kept in the loop.

A life sentence?

All I wanted was Rick out of our lives, convinced, for some stupid reason, that nothing really bad would happen to them. A slap on the wrist, at best. Maybe a stern talking to by somebody in charge: "You best be leaving those boys alone! Y'hear?"
I never pictured the old man rotting in a jail cell for the rest of his life.
"What about Misty Two?" Joey asked.
"Oh, she's fine. Mr. Shelton, your old neighbor, he has a friend who hunts and he's taking her in."
"That's cool," I said. "She's a bird dog after all."
From the DHR offices, we drove to a medical center on the other side of town.
"What are we doing here?" I asked in the parking lot.
"Need to get y'all checked out," Sandra said. "Make sure y'all healthy."
"We already had all our shots," I assured them. "We're cool."
"Don't worry. This is just normal procedure."
Normal procedure? I didn't like the sound of that. Neither did Joey. In the waiting room, he looked at me nervously. When we heard our names over the intercom, we went to our separate examination rooms. In mine, a young nurse with red hair handed me a blue gown, folded tight like a newspaper. Said, "Put this on."
I peeled off my jeans, wrapped the gown around me and sat on the table. Several minutes later, the door opened and a man in a white coat entered. He sat down on the stool and looked over my chart.
"How you doing, champ?"
I tried to tell him that I was fine, that I'd just been to the Navy hospital in Long Beach before we left California, that I'd gotten all my shots for the new school and that I didn't want any more needles stuck in me.
"No needles," the doc said with a chuckle. "This time

we're looking for something different."
The exam started off like all the other physicals I'd ever had: with the snap of translucent gloves. But there was no velcro strap around the pythons for the big squeeze, no icy chrome disk on my chest and back, no flashlight down the ole hatch and no Maxwell's rubber hammer. No, this exam consisted of only one test.
"Just roll over on your side and relax," the doctor said. "This won't take but a second."
"Is this absolutely necessary?" I asked desperately as I began to understand what was about to happen.
"Don't worry. You might feel some slight discomfort..."
Slight discomfort? I clenched my eyes shut and braced myself for the excrutiating pain that was about to shoot through my entire body. But just when I thought he was taking his sweet time about it, the doc pulled off the gloves and said, "Okay, you can get dressed now."
I thanked him absent-mindedly as he left the room.
Back in the waiting area, Joey was sitting next to the ladies. As we walked back to the van, I asked him, "How'd it go in there?"
"Okay."
"Yeah?"
"Yeah."
"He make you bend over and smile?" I laughed.
Joey looked away. "He didn't do that to you too?"
"Not even! He musta really liked you."
I laughed some more. Joey got that look like I'd socked him in the gut.
"Hey, as long as you didn't feel both his hands on your shoulders while he did the test you got nothing to worry about."
After that, I couldn't help but crack up.
From the medical center, we went to a drugstore. The ladies told us to get whatever we needed.
SHOPPING SPREE!
Joey and I each grabbed a basket and ran wildly through the store collecting items. I ended up with two spiral notebooks, a packet of Bics, Chapstick cause my lips were always dry, a bottle of Canoe and batteries for my walkman.
They even bought me a carton of cigarettes.
After stopping at McDonald's for lunch, we got on the interstate. With each mile between Anniston and Birmingham, my excitement increased. I listened to Black Flag on my headphones and stared out the window. There wasn't much to see as the van undulated through the rolling foothills. The scenery in Alabama never

seemed to change. Just a wall of pine trees
lining either side of the highway. An occasional
ridge covered in kudzu. A long narrow field of switch-
grass in the median.
   When we got closer to the city, the dense vegetat-
ion gave way to rows of blank homes, gas stations
and Waffle Houses. In the distance, I spotted a shopping center and traces of vehivcular congestion. The
outskirts of Birmingham offered a semblance of an
urban life I hadn't seen since we left LA. But just
as I was anticipating a view of the skyscrapers downtown, Sandra took the Eastlake exit and we drove through
a neighborhood with brick houses and manicured lawns
that looked exactly like Saks.
   Hillcrest Hospital was at the top of a hill. Hence
the name. It wasn't obvious at first that we were at
the funny farm, but as I watched Sandra and Clorise
fill out our forms, I figured it out. Still, what did
I know. Maybe being in the looney bin was like being
at camp.
   In the main office we were processed. Joey was
asigned to the youth ward and I was being put in the
adolescent ward. As soon as he realized we were getting split up, Joey started crying.
   "You said we were gonna stay together!" he bellowed
in the hallway, his voice bouncing off the walls.
   Clorise and Sandra looked at me and I stepped forward to calm him down.
   "It'll be cool." I socked him lightly in the arm.
"This is just temporary. It won't be so bad." I didn't
know what else to say. I was just as confused. We
had to trust the ladies. "Remember when we went to
camp as kids? We were in different cabins. This'll
be the same. Cool?"
   "You'll see your brother all the time," Clorise said
as she led him away. "Don't worry."
   Don't worry. Don't worry. They were like a broken
record, telling us all the time not to worry. But as
I followed Sandra through a set of double-doors that
separated the two wards, I couldn't help but expect
the worst.
   I was led into another room where a woman took my
bag and put my belongings into two piles: the things
I could keep and the questionable items that were
getting locked away. I groaned as my Walkman went into
the second pile. I'd only been able to listen to my
tapes for an hour and already I was back to a
life without tunes. I got to keep my notebooks, but
not the pens. How did that make any sense? I wanted
to protest but I bit my tongue. Then my carton of

Marlboros was added to the second pile and I couldn't hold back any longer.

"Smoking?" I asked.

"Not until you get to the second level," the woman responded.

"The second level? What's that?"

"You'll find all that out during your orientation tomorrow morning."

"Great, so I can't smoke till then?"

The woman ignored my question and pointed at my jacket. "Do you want to remove the pins or turn the whole thing over?"

"What? This is my jacket." I bristled at the thought but forced a smile. "Okay. It's cool. You can have the jacket."

"The earrings too. And the bandanas."

I grudgingly pulled out the loops and studs that lined both of my lobes and set them on the countertop. Then I untied the bandanas from around my legs.

"Are those safety pins in your jeans?"

"Yeah."

"I'm going to need your shoelaces as well."

I heaved a sigh. Was I going to end up buck naked by the time she was done confiscating all my shit? I wanted to hate the woman. But she had a kind face. Her face seemed to apologize, like her smile was trying to tell me that it was her job and she knew the whole process was stupid. But it had to be done. According to the nameplate over her left tit she was a psych tech. Her name was Rosie Fitzpatrick.

With that consoling smile, she put the rest of my things back into the bag.

"This way and I'll show you to your room."

I picked up my Hefty bag, lighter now with half my meager possessions confiscated, and followed Rosie down a hallway.

The room was like any other hospital room. Two bunks on either side and a small wardrobe in each corner. The one on the right was congested with books and toiletries, so I set my bag on the unoccupied bed.

"Everybody's in the common room," Rosie said. "Why don't you follow me there now."

As we walked down the hallway, I heard the chatter of multiple voices getting louder with each step. Rosie pushed open another double-door and we entered a large room with about thirty teenagers gathered in clusters on chairs and couches. At the far end was a pool table.

I scanned the faces that stared me down for potential threats and alliances. I noticed a guy with long hair wearing a Rush shirt at the pool table. My homemade anarchy shirt trumped his a million-fold, but I wasn't feeling picky.

"Children can I have your attention," Rosie said loudly. "This is Louis."

I blushed at the lackluster ripple of garbled acknowledgments and raised my hand--the guilty one. I stood in the center of the room for what felt like an eternity. Without my paraphernalia, I felt naked under the scrutiny. A few seconds later, the faces returned to reading magazines, playing board games and interrupted conversations. I casually wandered over to the pool table. Besides the guy in the Rush shirt, there were two other guys watching the game.

"How you doing?" the guy in the Rush shirt said.

"I'm Alex." He had a firm handshake. "I think we're gonna be roommates. I got the vacancy." From a distance, he looked older, like he was in his early twenties, but up close, his face was covered in acne and pockmarks that offset the thin patch of dark peach fuzz above his lip. "Where you from?"

"LA."

"They sent you here all the way from LA?"

"Nah," I laughed. "I've been living in Saks."

"You must be military."

"Yeah. How'd you know?"

"Why else would you be in Saks? Fort McClellan, right? I'm from Huntsville. Half the people there are military too." Alex pointed at the pool table. "Say, you wanna play doubles after this game?"

Even though I'd never played pool before and only had a vague understanding of the rules (I knew the balls were supposed to go in the pockets), I agreed and kept an eye on the current game to pick up some pointers.

Alex's opponent played skillfully. As he lined up his shots, he brushed the hair out of his face with the back of his hand. He wore a pink Izod shirt, plaid shorts and topsiders without socks.

At the other end of the table, a guy in track shorts and a tank top stood silently.

"Your shot," the prep yelled.

"Again?" Alex took the cue and perused his options. "I might just have a chance to beat your ass if you keep playing like that." He lined up the cue and the ball landed in a side pocket. "Sweet. Now watch me run the table." Alex moved to the next shot. He aimed and pulled back the cue, but the ball bounced off the edge of the pocket and clattered against the other balls on the table. "Crap on a stick. I suck at this

game. You any good?" he asked me.
"Not really." I didn't want to lie.
The guy in the track shorts walked over. Alex made the introductions. "This is Scott."
I shook his hand.
"So, what's it like in here?" I asked.
"Boring as all hell," Alex said. "Not much to do but play pool. There's some games and stuff like that." He nodded at some teenagers playing Risk. "Oh man!" Alex turned back to the pool table quickly. "Well, that's game right there."
"I kinda feel bad humiliating you all the time," the victor said as he approached smiling. "But not that bad."
"Ryan, this is Louis. He comes to us from LA via Saks. Louis, Ryan. He's from Mountain Brook. Nobody can beat him at pool."
"Billards is a game descended from French nobility," Ryan proclaimed grandiosely.
"Good to know," Alex rolled his eyes. "So man, you up for a game?"
"Sure."
It was Alex and me against Ryan and Scott. Just as I thought, I sucked at pool. It took me several attempts before I was even able to hit the cueball. Each time I tried to nail it, the end of the cue bounced off the side. Before I could get the hang of it, a heavyset black woman walked into the center of the room and announced in a roar that transcended all the other noise, "Supper time!"
"Coolness." Alex rubbed his hands together. "Time to moge."
Ryan and Alex followed a group of kids through the double-doors.
"Where're they going?" I asked Scott, the remaining player.
"Cafeteria. They're second level." Scott had a square jaw. His black hair was close-cropped on the sides and spiked on top. He moved with an athletic gait, but his deep-set eyes were full of confusion, darting left and right as he moved towards the other side of the room.
Two men in white coats pushed carts into the room and everybody gathered around them. On the carts were metal pans containing salisbury steaks in a thick brown goop, soggy french fries, corn niblets and green beans.
"Hey, it's a TV dinner without the tray," I joked as I sat down next to Scott. "Where's the cobbler?"
"Only people on second level get desert."

"So what do you hafta do to get on this second level?"
"Be perfect."
"What does that mean?"
Scott swallowed a mouthful of steak. "The point system is a game. But with all these twists. Just when you think you got it figured out, they pull a fast one and change it up. So, unless you're perfect, you can't win."
I had no idea what he was talking about but nodded like I did.
Around the long table, a flurry of conversation had erupted. Discussions intermingled with waves of laughter and the screeching girls. I examined the faces as furtively as possible. Three girls hovered together at the far end giggling. A redhead with a constellation of freckles smiled at me.
After the meal, I said aloud, "Man, I could really go for a smoke."
"On the second level you can smoke before coming back to the ward," Scott said.
"How come you know so much about the second level?"
"I've been on the second level already, but now I'm back on the first."
"What happened?"
"Ah, you know, every time I try to do something good, it messes up. But it's not my fault."
"Hey, man, I know what that's like."
"There are a lot of people here who want me to fail."
I pointed at the pool table to change the subject.
"Wanna play a game?"
Scott and I shared the cue. While we practiced shots, the redhead walked by and looked in our direction. She smiled.
"Hey, Louis. I'm Shirelle."
"What's up?" I smiled back.

When the second level returned from the cafeteria, Alex and Ryan joined us at the pool table.
"Who's up for another game of doubles?" Alex asked.
Ryan grabbed the cue. "Rack 'em!"
While we waited for our turns, Alex stood next to me. I could smell cigarette smoke on his clothes.
"You smoke?" I asked.
"Like a fiend," said Alex.
"I'm dying for a smoke," I thought if I kept saying it, somebody would eventually hand me a cigarette.
"The second level is mandatory for a steady intake of nicotine," Alex said.
"So what's the deal?" I asked. "How do I get on the second level?"

During the next game, the guys explained the level system to me. Everybody started off on the first level. To get to the second level, you collected points and when you had enough and had done everything by the book, they moved you up to the second level. I thought that since I hadn't actually done anything to warrant being there, I'd be on the second level in no time. When I pointed this out, Alex asked me the magical question: "So what brings you to Hillcrest?"

"Evaluation, they say." I remembered what I'd seen on the paperwork the ladies had filled out.

Ryan scoffed. "We're all in here for evaluations. That's just a word. It doesn't mean nothing. All that matters is your diagnosis."

"My what?" I asked.

"It's what they treat you for," Alex clarified. "Depression is the most popular diagnosis. There's Bobby over there, that guy Paul, Fred and Caroline... and I think Thomas too. According to their evaluations, they're all depressed."

"They don't seem that bummed out," I said.

"Exactly." Ryan handed Alex the cue. "Everybody's all perfectly cheerful when they don't have to deal with the bullshit at home and school. That's the joke. They come here all messed up, but within a few days, they're cool and it's like they've been cured. Then, they go home and the problems just start all over again."

"It's a total racket," said Scott.

Alex missed his shot. "Besides depression, suicide's another popular one. There's four of them right now. Besides Ryan."

"Oh yeah?" I was curious about the pool shark. He came off the most normal and sophisticated of the bunch.

"Ryan here is the suicidal prep." Alex referred to him as if he were on the chopping block. "Born poor, raised by his mom who worked two jobs to afford their apartment in Mountain Brook so he could attend the most elite school in Birmingham. But as much as he tried to fit in with the rich kids, he couldn't handle the pressure. So one day, he snapped. Drank a bottle of vodka and make spaghetti dinner of his wrists."

"That's fucked up." I looked at Ryan's arms and noticed the scars.

Alex pointed at three skinny girls sitting in a tight circle.

"See those chicks over there? The bulimic sisters. Everyday they're dressed up like they're going to

prom night in Ethiopia. But if they weight drops, they get put on feeding tubes."
"Gnarly."
"Whenever I look at their fingers, I can't stop thinking about how many times they've shoved them down their throats." Alex paused for several seconds and then shuddered. "The suicides and the depressed are way more fun to be around."
"What's the deal with her?" I pointed at a girl applying make-up on the couch. She had a large mane of curly blonde hair. Definitely the cutest girl in the room, acting like she knew it too.
"That's Cindy," Alex told me. "But don't even think about it."
"Miss fancy pants," Scott added. "She's so stuck up it's like she's got a rake up her butt."
"Plus, she's got the personality of a fence pole," said Ryan. "All she ever talks about is designer clothes, going on vacation, her father's Jag... She carries a BMW key around with her, but she's not even old enough to drive."
"What's her problem?" I asked.
"Besides the obvious? Nobody knows. It's all a big mystery how she made it to the second level."
"She's just a rich bitch," Scott said.
"Her parents have influence." Ryan took the cue from Alex. "Must be nice."
"My parents are just influenced," Alex quipped.
"So why are you here?" I asked Alex.
"Shit, I got busted for selling pot. Got me on a lousy dimebag. Can you believe that?"
"They didn't put you in jail?"
"At first, yeah. But then my lawyer convinced the judge that I was emotionally disturbed over my folks getting divorced, which is why I was using pot in the first place. So they sent me here for a psych review."
"How long ago was that?"
"Three months."
"Shit."
"Hey, it beats jail. I don't know what's gonna happen when I get back in front of the judge--they ain't been able to stick anything on me yet. But for now, it's smooth sailing."
"What about you, Scott?" I asked. "Why are you here?"
"Have you talked to Scott?" Ryan guffawed. "He's got a new problem every day. He's the screw up."
"Man, whatever," Scott mumbled. "It's my parents who are all messed up."
"Oh yeah, sure... that's just what a screw up would say." Ryan cracked up while Scott pouted. "So," Ryan

turned his attention to me. "You know who you're gonna be yet?"
"It's not like that for me," I said. "My parents didn't send me here. I had my father arrested. Me and my kid brother, that is."
"That's awesome," said Scott. "I wish I could send my dad to jail."
"We just moved here and we don't have any family around, so there's nowhere else for us to go. This is just a stop-off or something. I'll be out of here in no time." I saw their doubtful expressions. "Once I get my evaluation..." I laughed nervously.
Alex reached for the cue. "Well, you better hope your evaluation doesn't take as long as mine."

Later that night, the black woman from earlier walked back into the room and barked, "Quiet time!"
Her name was Vera. The guys had given me the rundown on the staff. Rosie was in charge and Vera was her second in command. There were several other psych techs, a whole army of them to keep tabs on us and make sure we did everything by the book.
I followed Alex back to the room. I was glad we ended up roommates.
As we lounged on our bunks, Alex told me, "I was worried when the last guy left. You never know who you're gonna get."
I pointed at the portable stereo on the table between our beds. "What kind of music do you listen to?"
"Here, check it out." Alex handed me a box of tapes.
I read off the titles: "Doors, Floyd, Zep. This is some good shit, but I'm mostly into thrash and punk." I listed off some of my favorite bands: Black Flag, Metallica, Anthrax, the Sex Pistols.
"Punk's cool," Alex said. "But this is where it all comes from." He showed me tape with a black cover.
I leaned in close to read the title. "Motorhead. Oh, man, I've been wanting to check them out!"
"Oh, we'll check them out alright. We're gonna be rocking some major tunage. For sure."
From the hallway came a bellowing command: "LIGHTS OUT!"
"Fucking hell, does she scream like that all the time?"
"Yeah. Vera's got a real set of pipes."
"She could front a metal band."
"No shit."

That night I was out with the lights.

CASE ACTION SUMMARY
—CRIMINAL

IN THE CIRCUIT COURT OF CALHOUN COUNTY

CC 87-860

Assigned to Judge: Street

Form C-6 / SENTENCING JUDGE: Street

Case Number CC— 87 860
ID — YEAR — NUMBER

[APPEAL FROM _____ COURT]

Fel / Jury / Non-Jury

DEFENDANT: [redacted]

CASE NUMBER CC— 87 860

OFFENSE (Charge):
I. Sodomy 13A-6-63
II. Sexual Abuse 13A-6-66

DATE FILED (DOCKETED) C.C.: 8-10-87

Grand Jury #: 252 **Date of Indict.:** 8-7-87

LOWER COURT NO

DEFENSE ATTORNEY(S): Steve Stephens — Ret./App.

PROSECUTING ATTORNEY: Morgan
(for State)
(for Mun.)

BLACK / x WHITE — MALE / FEMALE

DOB: 8-18-67

Occupation / Trade:

Defendant's Address: 5601 ____ Rd.

COURT INFORMATION

CAPIAS: D.C. Warrant / Mun. Warrant / G.J.-C.C. Writ

BOND: D.C. Bond / Mun. Bond / C.C. Bond

INITIAL APPEARANCE: DATE — D.C. / MUN. / C.C.

PRELIMINARY HEARING:

DEFENDANT STATUS: Pers. Bond / Prop. Bond / Surety / Co. Jail / City Jail / Prison

---

SHIT ON A SHINGLE

TO: ALABAMA BOARD OF CORRECTIONS — MONTGOMERY, ALABAMA — ATTN: CENTRAL RECORDS OFFICE.
IN RE: CONVICTION REPORT [EXCERPT-TRANSCRIPT OF OFFICIAL RECORD] OF DEFENDANT'S CONVICTION & SENTENCE.

SHIT ON A SHINGLE

Rick was psyched to the hilt when he pulled into the driveway. His first Training Camp had been a major adrenaline rush. Two weeks of battle exercises and faux-skirmishes on the endurance course at Fort Benning and he returned to the civilian world electrified.
 Even though his muscles ached from daily calisthenics, he felt rejuvenated, like he could climb a mountain without breaking a sweat.
 As he stepped out of the car whistling a tune, Rick heard yaps and howls from inside the house.
 "Joey! I'm home!" he called out, slightly peeved that his little man wasn't at the door to greet him, thinking maybe the boy was out back playing in the woods. There had to be a good reason why he didn't come running. But the puppy... the puppy was going berserk.
 "Somebody's happy I'm home," Rick said and chuckled. "Hold your horses, you little bitch!"
 Rick pushed the door open and the puppy accosted him with a frenzy of affection, bouncing off his legs and howling in glee.
 "Yeah, that's a good girl," Rick cooed and patted her head. "I'm happy to see you too. Where's Joey?"
 Inside the house, Rick winced at the acrid stench of dog piss.
 "Joey! Where the hell are you?" He sniffed the air and shouted louder, "Did you let the dog piss in the house again?" Then to himself, "Can't trust those kids with no..."
 In the hallway, Rick froze. His mind scrambled to make sense of the chaotic scene: the kitchen floor was covered with shards of glass, broken dishes, dented soup cans, ripped open boxes of cereal and hundreds of spaghetti strands spread out like pick-up sticks.
 "What the fuck?! Joey! JOEY! GODDAMN IT!"

Rick ran into the master bedroom and surveyed what was left of his many prized possessions. Bits of plastic and electronics were scattered everywhere. Cassettes snapped in half, the magnetic tape strewn about like wads of brown tinsel. Empty candybar wrappers and Doritos bags littered the floor. The shell of his Nintendo lay cracked on his pillow. The VCR was still on his dresser next to the TV, but there was a fist-sized impression in the top of the case.

Rick dashed frantically through the house with the puppy yapping at his heels. The entire place had been ransacked, as if a marauding gang of dervishes had come to visit. The only clue to what had happed was a message scrawled on the living room wall: "FEEL THE WRATH OF THE INNOCENTS!"

"LOUIS!" Rick yelled out the back door. "JOEY!" His voice echoed off the trees, but there was no response, just the constant cicada whine. "GODDAMN IT!" he seethed. "If you're hiding you better come out this instant! JOEY! LOUIS! I'm telling you, it'll be easier if you surrender!"

Rick started when he noticed Mr. Shelton standing on his patio next door.

"Where are those damn kids?" Rick demanded as he approached his neighbor. "Have you seen what they've done to the house? I'm going to kill them! Oh, I swear, I'm going to kill them!"

"You ain't doing nothing to those boys no more." Mr. Shelton stood with his arms crossed. He appeared calm but his voice cracked with indignation.

"What are you talking about?" Rick replied, dumbfounded. "No, they're going to pay for what they've done. You should see the place! They wrecked it! And where were you? You were supposed to keep an eye on them! The house is trashed! Trashed!"

"Them boys ain't around for you to mess with no more."

Rick felt a chill go down his spine. "What are you talking about?"

"You heard me."

"What?" Rick shook his head in disconnect. "Where are the boys?"

"They're gone. The state got 'em."

"The state? What the hell are you talking about?"

"They know what y'all been doing over there." Mr. Shelton could no longer contain his disgust. "Damn perverts."

Rick returned the man's ire. "You have no right to talk to me this way! I'm a soldier! I serve my country! We asked you to keep an eye on them and this is the job you do? I'm calling the cops!"

"Call them," Mr. Shelton snarled. "They be happy to hear from you, I reckon." He walked back to his house. Confused and angry, Rick shouted, "I want those kids! Tell me where they are! You can't do this! You have no right!" He stood his ground but after a few moments, alone with his fury, he gave up.
On the way back to the house, he slammed the back door and punched the kitchen wall as hard as he could. His knuckles burst open and blood ran down his fingers. But he didn't feel a thing, too wrapped up with the riddle of Mr. Shelton's comments. As blood dripped from his trembling fingertips onto the linoleum floor, he kicked a can of beans that rolled under the table. The puppy chased after it and returned for another round of fetch. Snatching the phone out of the cradle, Rick dialed and waited. "Goddamn it, Claude... Pick up..." After ten rings, he slammed the phone down and punched the wall with his other fist.
"Fuck!" Rick sat down on a chair and lit a cigarette. The blood soaked into the paper as he inhaled.
Eventually, the puppy calmed down and curled up on his boot.

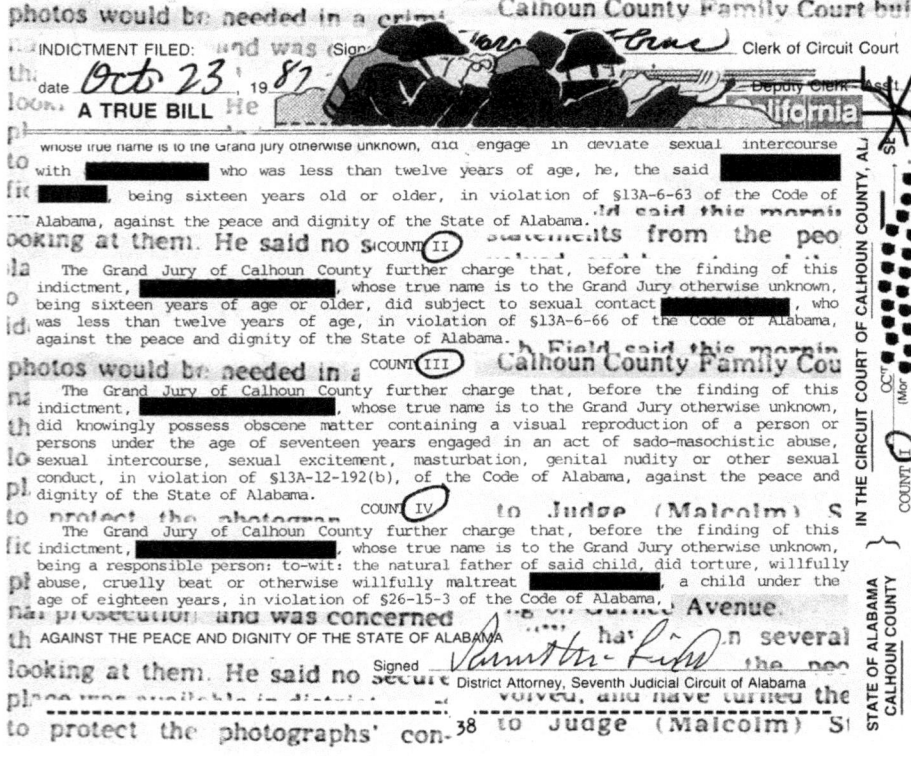

38

✳ In line at the Winn-Dixie,
            Claude surveyed
      the contents in his shopping cart:
                    a package of chicken,
barbecue sauce, a can of black-eyed peas and a
box of Cotton Pickin' cornbread mix. He was looking
forward to the meal he planned to make that evening.
After ten days of C-rations and chipped beef at the
Scarf and Barf, he had a taste in his mouth so sour
it wouldn't go away no matter how many cigarettes
he smoked. They didn't call it shit on a shingle for
nothing, he thought with a slight chuckle.
   The cashier smiled at him.
   "How are things going today, Laurie?" Claude knew
her name from the nametag on her red and green smock.
He spoke with flirtatious tones, an old man in uniform.
   "Oh, alright," she said. "Ready to be home with the
kids." Laurie returned his pleasantries. "Looks like
it's gonna be good eatin' for y'all." She nodded at
the items moving down the conveyor belt.
   "Oh, yes." Claude sighed.

"Been two weeks
        in the
              field
                  and it's time
                          for a decent meal."

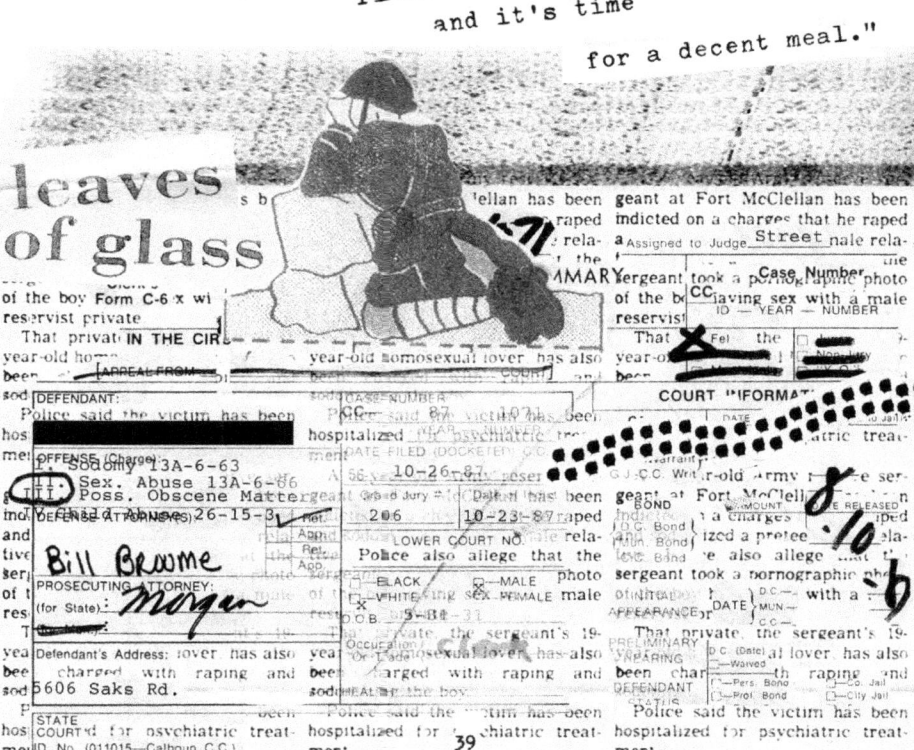

"I bet."

Claude glanced at the candy display and wondered how much hell the boys had raised while they were home alone. What will the neighbors say? Louis was always up to no good, encouraging his brother to do the same. Since he was a child, it was one thing after another. Louis was almost sixteen, but he acted like a petulant child. It wasn't like they had a choice but to leave him unsupervised.

"Is this gonna be it?" Laurie asked.

"Two packs of Kools," Claude said and picked up a bag of M&Ms and a Three Musketeers. "These too."

After a little banter about how hot it had been so far that summer, Claude took his two bags and headed home. The grocery store was only a mile from the house but he lit a cigarette anyway. As he parked, he kept it balanced between his lips, then while he pulled out the bags and walked through the front door.

"Hello!" he shouted and smoke spewed from the end of the Kool. The puppy ran to him with an excited whimper, clawing at his pantsleg. "Anybody home? I got groceries." He made his way down the hallway, juggling the bags as he reached to pull the cigarette from his mouth and almost dropped one when he entered the kitchen. Surrounded by the mess, Rick was sitting in the middle of the room, his hand covered in blood.

"What the..." It was all Claude could muster.

"This is how I found it." Rick's voice was monotone.

Claude set the bags on the table and snapped at the puppy. "Down! Now!" Then to Rick, "Where are the boys?"

"Gone."

Claude was more alarmed by Rick's reticence than the condition of the house. "Gone?"

"Gone." Rick lit a Marlboro.

"What the fuck does that mean?"

"Ask the redneck next door?"

"Shelton?"

"All he said was the state took them."

"The state?"

Rick took a drag from the cigarette. "Yeah."

"I'm getting to the bottom of this right now."

Claude went out the back door, pushing the puppy back when she tried to follow him.

Mrs. Shelton answered the door. "Claude, I'm sorry," she said. Her brow was furrowed with concern.

"What's going on, Mabel?"

"I don't know what to say," she whispered. "What you've done... the photographs..." She held her head down, unable to finish the sentence.

"What photographs?" Claude asked.
"The boys gave them to the social workers."
"The social workers came back? Why?"
Mrs. Shelton opened her mouth but before she could say anything, her husband walked up behind her.
"We said all we're gonna say." He closed the door.
Claude stood there for a few seconds before he returned to the house. His pace quickened as he moved past Rick, stepped over the jetsam and ignored the barking dog. He went straight into his bedroom, pulled open the top drawer of his dresser and rifled through the contents, tossing things onto the floor as he searched. When he realized the polaroids were gone, he closed the drawer slowly.
Holding himself upright with his hands on the side of the dresser, he marveled at how the amber glow of the sunlight coming through the window radiated on the wood grain. It was late afternoon, but the sun was taking its sweet time. The room was boiling, he noticed. Sweat beaded on his forehead. They had planned to buy an air-conditioner when they got back from Camp Benning. Been talking about it for a while... There were some good deals down at the Wal-Mart...
"They're your kids. They can't just take them away like this."
Rick was standing in the doorway. His voice penetrated Claude's fugue. He turned and saw Rick's lips move, but he couldn't make out the words. The ringing in his ears grew louder as it pulsated in his skull.
"I... uh..." Claude lunged through the door and pushed Rick aside. He barely made it to the bathroom before he fulfilled the promise of the Scarf and Barf. Collapsed over the commode, a piece of plastic piercing his knee, he felt Rick's presence.
He was still talking.

The puppy wasn't giving up an inch.

His head was spinning.

But his only thought was,

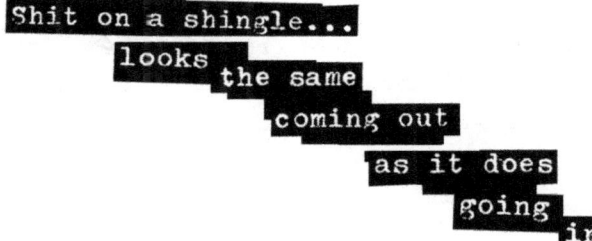

Shit on a shingle... looks the same coming out as it does going in.

| GRAND JURY DOCKET No. 2 06 | INDICTMENT (General) | CIRCUIT COURT No. CC 87-1071 ID - Yr. - Number |

STATE OF ALABAMA
CALHOUN COUNTY } IN THE **CIRCUIT** COURT OF **CALHOUN** COUNTY, ALABAMA

COUNT **I** OCTOBER (Month) , SESSION, 19 **87**

The Grand Jury of **Calhoun** County charge that, before the finding of this Indictment . . . .

whose true name is to the Grand jury otherwise unknown, did engage in deviate sexual intercourse with ███████ who was less than twelve years of age, he, the said ███████, being sixteen years old or older, in violation of §13A-6-63 of the Code of Alabama, against the peace and dignity of the State of Alabama.

COUNT **II**

The Grand Jury of Calhoun County further charge that, before the finding of this indictment, ███████, whose true name is to the Grand Jury otherwise unknown, being sixteen years of age or older, did subject to sexual contact ███████, who was less than twelve years of age, in violation of §13A-6-66 of the Code of Alabama, against the peace and dignity of the State of Alabama.

COUNT **III**

The Grand Jury of Calhoun County further charge that, before the finding of this indictment, ███████, whose true name is to the Grand Jury otherwise unknown, did knowingly possess obscene matter containing a visual reproduction of a person or persons under the age of seventeen years engaged in an act of sado-masochistic abuse, sexual intercourse, sexual excitement, masturbation, genital nudity or other sexual conduct, in violation of §13A-12-192(b), of the Code of Alabama, against the peace and dignity of the State of Alabama.

COUNT **IV**

The Grand Jury of Calhoun County further charge that, before the finding of this indictment, ███████, whose true name is to the Grand Jury otherwise unknown, being a responsible person; to-wit: the natural father of said child, did torture, willfully abuse, cruelly beat or otherwise willfully maltreat ███████, a child under the age of eighteen years, in violation of §26-15-3 of the Code of Alabama,

AGAINST THE PEACE AND DIGNITY OF THE STATE OF ALABAMA

Signed _____
District Attorney, Seventh Judicial Circuit of Alabama

A TRUE BILL

Signed _W.E._____
FORELADY-FOREMAN

NO -or- _____, Prosecutor

Indictment received in Open Court by Judge from Foreman (Forelady) in presence of at least 11 other Grand Jurors.

Bond Set at $ 50,000

Signed _____
JUDGE

INDICTMENT FILED:
date **Oct 23**, 19 **87**

Signed _R. Forrest_____ Clerk of Circuit Court

I WANA FIND SOMETHING
I DIDN'T KNOW I HAD TO LOSE
I JUST NEED AN EXCUSE

I reserve the right to be miserable, and I'll take all those inconvenient obstacles, cause when you'r living in the city, the only uncontested path is a ride to the hospital.

I tried to leave it all behind
When I wiped the sleep from my eyes
But it come out from under
Beneath the haze of slumber

"THESE THINGS"
This is the one
I didn't throw away
I kept it where
it could be safe
inside your heart   ~~I kept it locked up~~
it was secure   ~~I kept it shut~~
cause you'd never
realize
how spectacular
~~it was~~   it could and
~~and if pre-dit~~   one day
              just might be
it's got nothing to do
with your perception of use
you can try all you want
to bum me out
but I got you pause
there's nothing left to talk about

I kept it locked up
I kept ~~IT Shut~~

Joey stared into his bowl of oatmeal. Around the table, his fellow Youth Ward residents talked loudly and giggled nonstop. Fucking morons, he thought, Happy as pigs in shit. Brainwashed and stupid.

Joey did not join their revelry. As he contemplated the lumpy gruel in front of him, he noticed a group of teenagers enter the cafeteria like a raucous mob. Joey perked up in anticipation. He scanned their faces as they collected trays and formed a disorderly queue at the serving stations. They laughed and horsed around while they ordered food and then sat down at tables on the other side of the dining room. When it was clear that Louis was not in their ranks, Joey's heart sank. Why isn't he eating breakfast with the other kids his age? he wondered desperately. Is he just late? Or have they taken him someplace else? You could never tell with those ladies... Gooks lie.

Joey stabbed the oatmeal with his spoon and twisted the handle. Those ladies, they sure pulled a fast one. They weren't supposed to have separated him and Louis. That was the deal. From the beginning, the ladies had promised to keep Joey and his brother together. That's why they gave them the polaroids. That's why they turned their father in. That's why they let the ladies take them away from home, away from everything they knew. But wasn't it just like a gook to say anything to get what they wanted? Surely, they wouldn't be able to trick Louis so easily. He was probably in another part of the building planning their escape. Louis wouldn't stand for this kind of treatment. Louis knew how to beat the gooks at their own game. That's what he said, back in the shelter: Don't worry. I won't let them pull any shit. It's you and me now. We'll get them to do whatever we want.

It just had to be true, Joey thought. It just had to.

Joey considered the last twenty four hours, cataloguing what he remembered... At first, there was the old lady at the shelter... Mrs. Gertie... Then Ricky Ricardo tricked Lucy--she thought he was letting her join the band, when really he had something else up his sleeve... But what? Who knows. That's when the gooks showed up. The fatso and the bimbo. They ruined everything. As shitty as that place was, being at the shelter with Louis was better than being here. For a second, it seemed like things were gonna get better. They took them to the store and let them buy whatever they wanted. But there was only junk at that store. No cool clothes, no cool games, just junk! And they owed us. Louis said we were getting a reward, but so far all they got was finger fucked by a guy in a white suit. Didn't even buy us dinner first, that's what Louis said. Fucked without a kiss... Like always. Like gooks. Just like gooks.

But there was the candybar on the ride to Birmingham. Joey smiled when he thought of that. Being in the back seat with his brother again... The Baudrey Boys ride again... That's what Louis said one night. He said, just you wait, nobody fucks with the Baudrey Boys. Then everything went FUBAR. As the van struggled up the circular driveway to the hospital, Louis said, I guess that's why they call it hillcrest. And then the filthy gooks cut the platoon in half. On the elevator they had the guts to say, You can still talk to your brother whenever you want. They promised. Just like they always did. Never trust a gook. They lie and trick you into the prison camp, thinking it'll only be for a short while... but you know all their methods of deception. They get you in the cage and then they lock the door.

Fucking gooks.

Now that Joey was captured by the enemy, all he had left for guidance was the code of conduct. He knew the code well. They all did. It was part of their training. His original orders were to follow the chain of command. Until he received new orders, he would remain combantant except when it was in his best interest to go along with the demands of his captors. When they ask questions, he will only give his name, rank and serial number.

Those were his orders.

And even then, the gooks wanted to confuse him. But he had trained for years, and now that he was on his first solo mission, he would use those skills to survive. Until Louis came to his rescue.

On the first day of his captivity, a hideous ogre, the queen gook, tried to get him to sign a confession.
"My name is Katrina." She smiled to hide the lies. "I need to ask you some questions." She tapped her pen against a clipboard full of papers that held all the lies. The gook lies.
She tried to act like they were old friends, just having a little chat. But Joey saw right through the act. He only had two questions: How long am I going to be here? And, Where is my brother?
But the tricky gook, she just kept saying, "We need to go over some things first."
Joey sat glumly on the edge of his bed, resolved to keep his mouth shut, like he'd been trained. Do what you want, but I ain't no snitch.
While the woman goaded him with her dastardly gook tricks, a curly-haired boy entered the room and stood next to other bed.
"Joey, this is Billy," she said. "He's your roommate."
"Hey, I'm Billy."
Joey looked at the other prisoner and knew right away that he was a stoolpigeon. He could see it in his stoolie eyes, his stoolie pipsquak voice. They were going to use him to get information. But Joey was too smart to fall for such an obvious gook trick.
"I'll just let you two get acquainted," the woman said as she walked out the door.
Billy stared at Joey. "This is my room."
Joey shrugged.
"I was here first. This is my room."
"Whatever, kid."
"This is my room."
Joey stared at the floor and tried to ignore the kid who kept repeating the same thing. Is this all you got? he thought. What kind of scheme is this? Annoy me into spilling my guts?
"Did you hear me?" Billy asked. "I said, This is my room."
"You keep saying that, shit-for-brains. But I don't care. So just shut up!"
Joey curled up on his bed and faced the wall. Deep in enemy territory, his mission was clear. Remain combatant until Louis gave him new orders. That was the chain of command. That was the code of conduct. That was all he knew.

That night, after we'd trashed everything in sight, we grabbed the Polaroid camera and ~~documented~~ our handywork. ~~And~~ And then, a portrait of the two of us, so there was no mistaking who was behind the wreckage

From the Notebook Lyrics of Louis Baudrey

"I forgot to tell you the most important part of group. You gotta get here early if you want a good seat." "Why?" "Cause, man, group's a total freak show."

I woke up the next morning and stared at the cottage cheese ceiling. If I squinted just right it could be the surface of the moon. The light was dim through the tinted plexiglass. I leaned over. Alex was reclined on his bed with a tattered paperback. I read the title: Breakfast of Champions.
"What's up?" I asked. "You studying for the big test?"
"Check it out." Alex held the book open to a page with a drawing of a large asterisk. "It's an asshole."
I laughed and then coughed. "Man, I need a cigarette."
"I remember when I first got here and couldn't smoke. It was torture."
"You got any tips on how I can get to the second level as fast as possible?"
Alex pondered the question before he replied.
"Talk." He paused to let me absorb this sage advice. "It doesn't matter what you say, as long as you say something. Talk. That's the name of the game. And the best place to talk is in group."
"Group?"
"Group's a breeze. Every day after breakfast we gather in a circle with this guy Ron and talk about our feelings and why we're here. It's all a buncha bullshit, but if you wanna get points, you gotta talk in group. So it's always good to have something to talk about. Otherwise you have to make something up on the spot, which might seem easy, but, trust me, it's not. That guy Ron's no schlub. He'll make you sweat. The best thing to do is what I do: give people advice. Add in a dash of insight from your own perspective-- anything to be part of the discussion. That's what they're looking for."
There was a knock on the door and Rosie walked in without any further warning. "Time to line up for the cafeteria," she told Alex.
"Smoke one for me, dude."

I joined the rest of the first level in the common room. On the pushcarts were large pans of scrambled eggs, bacon, grits and biscuits. Arranged on the table were jugs of orange juice and milk. I piled some eggs, bacon and a couple biscuits onto my plate and sat down next to Scott.

"I'm so sick of scambled eggs." Scott stuck his fork into a pile of grits with a crater of melted butter on top.

"I know, they're all runny and gross. Bacon's alright though."

"In the cafeteria you can get omelets, hashbrowns, pancakes and waffles..."

"Scott, all you do is complain." A guy sat down and introduced himself as he shoveled a forkful of eggs into his mouth. "Larry's the name, being crazy's the game." He laughed heartily and specks of food flew across the table. "Welcome to the adolescent ward."

"Thanks," I said and discreetly brushed a piece of egg from my arm. "How long you been here?"

"Two weeks. An eternity, it feels like. Be a whole lot better when I'm on the second level though. Getting the bump any day now. All my ducks are in a row."

"I guess if you're on the second level it isn't so bad here, huh?"

"Oh, sure. The doors are locked, the windows are thick plexiglass, we got video cameras aimed at us all the time and techs watching our every move... But yeah, as long as you can eat in the cafeteria, it's pretty awesome being locked up." His sarcasm was obvious enough without laughter, but Larry let out a snort to prove his point.

"So what're you in for?"

"I'm a Jew. In Alabama. Do the math." Larry glanced at me knowingly. "Not that being a Jew is reason for getting locked up anymore. I'm here cause I beat this guy up. Actually, I almost killed him. He used to always pick on me, making cracks about Nazis and all that stuff. One day I just snapped. When they pulled me off him, I was bashing his head into a metal door. Didn't even know what I was doing. I'd totally blacked out. So they sent me here to find out if it'll ever happen again. So... watch out!" Larry chuckled and more bits of egg scattered onto the table.

After breakfast, everybody began to gather on the couches and chairs. Alex waved me over to where he was seated.

"Hey, I saved you a spot," he said cheerfully. "I forgot to tell you the most important part of group. You gotta get here early if you want a good seat."

"Why?" I asked.

Smiling wide, Alex leaned in close and whispered, "Cause, man, group's a total freak show."

When Ron entered, the collective roar of chatter went dead. Ron sat down in the empty chair reserved for him and asked, "How's everyone doing today?"

He received a weak ripple of salutations.

"Let's see..." Ron scanned the faces and asked, "Who haven't we heard from lately... How about you, Jasper?"

A guy with curly brown hair perked up.

"The last time we heard from you I believe you were talking about feeling isolated from your family and your schoolmates. Have you gained any new perspectives on that?"

Jasper sighed. "Yeah. I've learned that I have a problem making friends because I expect too much out of folks and I never give anybody a chance." Jasper talked reluctantly, his tone forced and his words practiced.

"How do you feel about going home and dealing with your parents and school again?"

"I'm trying to be more assertive and less defensive with my parents. Since they're just trying to help me. And I'm gonna try to not be so distrustful of people at school."

"Very good, Jasper. I'm happy to hear that. Who wants to go next?" Ron paused and looked the group over. "Gloria, why don't you tell us why you're here."

Gloria heard her name and sat up straight. "Well, I'm at Hillcrest cause my mother don't like me dating a black boy. A few weeks ago, she was tidying up my room--you know, being a nosey nelly--and found a stack of letters from my boyfriend that I'd hidden in the back of my closet. At first she was happy that I'd found somebody, but also hurt I hadn't told her about him before. She kept asking me about Quentin--that's his name--and I kept putting her off, coming up with any excuse why she couldn't meet him. Even though I knew what she'd say, I eventually told her the truth. Shoot, I figured when she found out my boyfriend was black she'd have a cow, but she not only had a cow, she had a sheep, a goat, a pig and a chicken. And then she sent me here. Said I needed to get it out of my system." Gloria shook her head. "I love my momma, but I think she ain't right being a bigot."

"We don't always agree with our parents," Ron said.

"It don't matter none... Soon as I get outa here, I'm getting back together with Quentin. It ain't nobody's business who I date."

"Well, let's hope that you and your mother can both learn to respect each other's differences and find some common ground."

The room was quiet for a few minutes in honor of the star-crossed lovers. Then Ron cleared his throat.

"Shirelle, why don't you go next."

"I'm here cause I'm broken," Shirelle said, matter-of-fact. "And they still haven't figured out how to fix me."

"We've talked about this before, Shirelle. Why do you feel the need to label yourself?"
"Cause everybody thinks I'm crazy. People always say I want some of what she's on. But I tell 'em, I'm just doing my thang, you know? People say that girl's not right in the head. But I just say, y'all can suck my ass." She chortled loudly.
"Is it really important what others think?"
"It ain't. I'm just telling you what they say. I don't give two sh--I mean, I don't care. They're all stupid anyway. They call me crazy when I'm doing my thang, but when I'm quiet and just thinking about stuff, they say I'm depressed. Everybody thinks one thing or another... Shoot, I got a list of what people be calling me."
"Is skank on the top of that list?" asked Cindy.
"Suck my ass!" Shirelle snapped. "You think you so special, acting all highfaluting. But you from Leeds, and Leeds ain't no Lifestyles of the Rich and Famous."
"Least I ain't no skank."
"Let's try to be civil, ladies," Ron said. "Shirelle, what is it about Cindy's attitude that bothers you?"
"I just don't like these girls who think they're so high and mighty, putting on airs like they're better'n everybody else. Cindy's just a bitch in a pretty dress. And that don't make her special."
"As if you could even afford a dress that wasn't made out of an Alpo bag."
"Ah, hell no!" Shirelle stood up and raised her fists.
The group oohed and ahhed at the potential action.
Ron tried to restore order. "Shirelle! Please take your seat. You know where that behavior will get you."
"Yeah, you're not being very assertive," Cindy said with a snicker as she leaned back in her chair.
"Don't aggravate her, Cindy," said Ron. "Shirelle, I'm asking you to please calm down. This is not how we communicate with each other."
Shirelle sat down and pointed her finger at Cindy. "If we weren't in here, I'd turn your ass inside out, take a picture and mail it to your grandma."
"In your dreams, potty mouth."
"Girls!" Ron raised his voice. "This is unacceptable behavior."
Rosie emerged from the nurses' station. "Do we have a problem in here?" Her voice carried such a commanding resonance that she didn't even have to yell to get her point across.
"No, ma'am," Shirelle and Cindy said meekly.
"Then I suggest you settle down."

"Yes, ma'am," they said again in unison.

"Now, let's try to stay focused on constructive comments only," Ron said. "Cindy, if you have a problem with the way Cindy is acting, you should try to be more courteous in your approach. Maybe you can help each other. It's important to learn from your peers and express yourself without fear of ridicule. That's what group is for. This is your forum, but we can't have name-calling and insults." Ron let us soak up his words before he continued. "Does anybody have something constructive they'd like to share?"

"I have a question," Alex said.

"Yes, Alex."

"What would a chair look like if our legs bent the other way?"

We all cracked up.

"Settle down, people. Alright, thank you, Alex, for that insightful contribution." Ron kept a straight face. "I think that's all the time we have today."

On the way back to our room, Alex told me, "And that was group. Best way to spend an hour when you got nothing else to keep you entertained."

✳ ✳ ✳

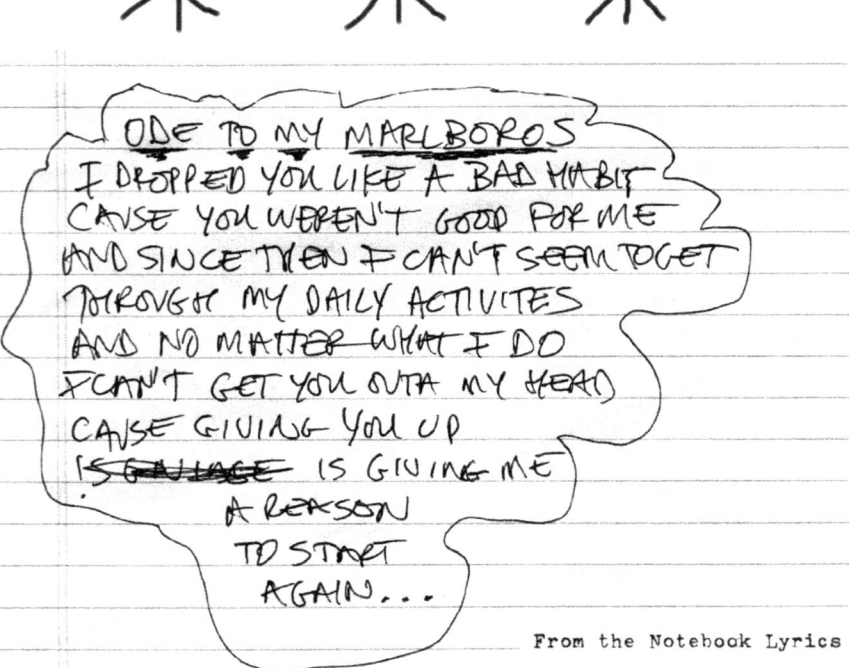

ODE TO MY MARLBOROS
I DROPPED YOU LIKE A BAD HABIT
CAUSE YOU WEREN'T GOOD FOR ME
AND SINCE THEN I CAN'T SEEM TO GET
THROUGH MY DAILY ACTIVITES
AND NO MATTER WHAT I DO
I CAN'T GET YOU OUTA MY HEAD
CAUSE GIVING YOU UP
IS ~~GARBAGE~~ IS GIVING ME
A REASON
TO START
AGAIN...

—— From the Notebook Lyrics

SECOND HAND PERSONALITY

We are all every one of us
disconnected revolving
satellites
We sit in a circle and
broadcast the daily fiction
of our private lies
But if I could categorize
a constant state of
mind I'm in
with a second hand
personality
I just might fit in
And I gotta get out
of this skin I'm in
find me something
a little better
to believe in...

CASE ACTION SUMMARY — CRIMINAL

CC 87-860 Assigned to Judge **Street**

Form C-6

IN THE CIRCUIT COURT OF CALHOUN COUNTY

Case Number CC— 87 860

[APPEAL FROM _____ COURT]

☒ Fel ☐ Jury
☐ Non-Jury
☐ Mun. ☐ Y.O.

DEFENDANT: ~~(redacted)~~

OFFENSE (Charge):
I. Sodomy 13A-6-63
II. Sexual Abuse 13A-6-66

DEFENSE ATTORNEY(S): Stev Stephens

PROSECUTING ATTORNEY (for State): Morgan

Defendant's Address: 5606 Saks Rd.

STATE COURT ID. No. (011015—Calhoun C.C.)

CASE NUMBER CC— 87 860
DATE FILED (DOCKETED) C.C. 8-10-87
Grand Jury # 252 **Date of Indict.** 8-7-87
LOWER COURT NO.
☐ BLACK ☒ MALE
☒ WHITE ☐ FEMALE
D.O.B. 8-18-67
Occupation / Or Trade:
HEALTH:

COURT INFORMATION

CAPIAS — D.C. Warrant / Mun. Warrant / G.J.-C.C. Writ

BOND — D.C. Bond / Mun. Bond / C.C. Bond

INITIAL APPEARANCE — DATE D.C. / MUN / C.C.

PRELIMINARY HEARING — D.C. (Date) / Waived

DEFENDANT STATUS — Pers. Bond / Prof. Bond / Pers. Recog / Co. Jail / City Jail / Prison

ARRESTING OFFICER — County / State / Conserv. / Mun

EXAMINERS (AUDIT) NOTES
Date — Initials — Note

☐ GUILTY PLEA BEFORE INDICTMENT ☒ YOUTHFUL OFFENDER

DATE(S)	ACTION (FILINGS/ORDERS)	MINUTES Bk. / Pg.
	Nolle Prosequi — Morgan	— / —
	(Note: See file or other sheets for possible entries) (Judges initials)	
8/19/87	Arraigned. "Not Guilty" Plea. Trial set: 9/14, 1987 9 A.M. (JHM)	
	See separate sheet for formal sentencing, etc.	
9-2-87	Petition for Treatment as a Youthful Offender	
9-2-87	Motion to Amend Plea	
9-18-87	Motion for Consolidation of Defendants — Order Setting hearing 9-21-87 at 4:30 pm — copies to Atty. Stephens & DA	
9-21-87	Deft. present with atty. S. Stephens, Carolyn Morgan appearing for State. After argument, the Court granted State's motion to consolidate for trial with CC-87-861, State vs. Dossit. Said ruling subject to...	

THE HANGED MAN

...der the Constitutions of the United States and of the State o...
...ence against yourself. In the trial of your case before the jury...
...lf, **In the trial of your case** require you to so testify...
...ne can even comment to the jury as to your failure to...
...ntarily say, with knowledge of your rights, may be us...
...ama you have a right or ... to be compel...
...ve the right to take the wit... nd to testify or...
...fy, you can be cross-examined by the state. If you do...
...ve the right to remain absolutely silent, but anythir...
...u. Your conversations with your attorney are confidential...
whether you are guilty plea of not guilty, and the righ...
...ine whether you are guilty or whether you are innocent, b...
lic tr... ry. In a jury trial, the jury wo...
...e tr... **HANGED** ...ey could subpoena witness...
ionable, cross-examine the witnesses of the state, examine...
to do everything that **to remain absolutely silent,**...
witnesses subpoenaed to testify as to pertinent facts in yo...
our behalf, make legal objections to matters that he felt v...
...n **you have a right** the matter before the jury. He woul...
...that you obtain a fair and impartial trial. You have the rig...
...e tri... of your case, you will co... clothed with...
II follo... u throughout the course... **MAN** ...til the eviden...
our... The burden of proof is upon the State of Alabama to...
...d witnesses doubt before the jury would be autho...
...iry's duty to find you not guilty. You will have no b...
...at you are not guilty and this presumption of innoce...
...he state convinces each juror beyond a reasonable d...
...and **duty to find you not guilty.** he case, that you...
...d you guilty. If the state does not meet such burden of pro...
...the charges set forth in the indictment you have the right t...
er **a fair and impartial trial.** plea of guilty only if you are...
EAD GUILTY THERE WILL BE NO JURY TRIAL, AS HAS BEEN H
LEAD GUILTY THERE WILL BE NO JURY TRIAL reason of insanity
PLEAD GUILTY THERE WILL BE NO JURY TRIAL NO JURY TRIA
LEAD GUILTY THERE WILL BE NO JURY TRIAL BE NO JURY TRI
EAD GUILTY THERE WILL BE NO PLEAD GUILTY THERE WILL B
THERE WILL BE PLEAD GUILTY THERE WILL BE NO JURY TRIA
GUILTY THERE WILL BE PLEAD GUILTY THERE WILL BE NO JU

For weeks, Claude had been taking the long way home from work, driving out of his way to prolong the inevitable. At first, he only went ten or twenty miles past his turnoff before making a u-turn. But lately he'd been going further north, to Gadsden and then Ft. Payne. Once, he even crossed into Georgia, but he turned around at the first exit, his heart beating in his ears. If a state trooper pulled him over, it was straight to the slammer. During that first interview with the police, they had made it clear: don't leave the area.

These solitary drives were his only refuge. Alone in the car, Claude felt at ease. If just for a short while he could imagine a reality different from the one he had no other choice but to accept. With the country station on the radio (there was no classical music on the dial in small town Alabama) and one of steady chain of Kools smoldering between his fingers, Claude reveled in the fantasy of escape. He imagined himself a fugitive, for the fun of it--why not? He looked at the world with a swindled taste of freedom. He absorbed the landscape--the piney rolling hills and red clay embankments--along the highway in the fading amber glow of the setting sun. Then night snuffed out the day and the only distraction left on the road were the periodic spectacles of well-lit gas station/mini-mart complexes.

At times, he fantasized about taking off into the unknown. It was a tempting idea. Soon concrete and iron would separate him from the rest of the world. And then, he could only think of the future. The police were coming to take him away. That much he knew for sure. But when, he had no clue. They could be on their way to pick him up at that very moment. And if not today, tomorrow. Or the day after that. On and on, it was all speculation. Until the day finally arrived.

The certainty was a switchblade in his gut.

At night, Claude barely slept a wink. His mind churned like a steam engine, fueled with the fear of arrest and the stifling heat that filled the house. He tried to drink himself into a stupor, but the whisky did little to mitigate the insomnia. In a daze, he half-slept, his thoughts entwined with the sound of Rick raging and lamenting his fate in the next room, cussing and occasionally punching the wall. Once Rick settled down, every speck of noise was a klaxon piercing the still night. On the nightstand, his watch ticked like marching feet. In the distance, a dog barked. Is that a posse or a lynch mob? Even the breeze rustled through the trees with the sound of official tiretread on the chert driveway.

Often, Claude imagined how it would go down when the police finally arrived. Would they be in uniforms? Regular cops on the beat? Or detectives in plainclothes. Would there be two? Four? Five? Six? The entire force? How many cops did they have in a town like Anniston? There would be handcuffs, of course. They'd read him his miranda rights and the the perp walk to the car. The ride downtown to the jailhouse.

The procedure played out in his head on repeat. It was all he thought about anymore. He excavated memories of prison movies and descriptions from books. The myth and mystique of hard time was all he had to go on since he'd never actually talked to an ex-con before. Unlike Rick, who resisted his fate, Claude hoped that if he prepared himself mentally for prison, when it actually happened, the reality wouldn't be as disturbing as it seemed to him with the last traces of freedom hanging like a loose thread.

In the meantime, Claude maintained his daily activities. He got out of bed each morning and put on his uniform. It was hard to shave without looking at himself in the mirror, but after a cup of instant coffee, he stepped outside and quickly walked to his car, hoping to avoid a confrontation with the neighbors. He saw judgement in every face he encountered. There wast much he could do to stop the repercussions.
Rums abounded in a small town as the locals sought justice through a vicious smear campaign.

One night, Claude and Rick were in the kitchen when a rock crashed through the window. Rick fell to the floor while the puppy yapped madly.
Claude hardly flinched, picked up the rock, on which "GET OUT" had been scrawled, and tossed it back out. It landed with a pathetic thud in the yard.

It was summer, but the field behind the house, where the neighbor kids usually played, was eerily absent of any gleeful cries or high-pitched squeals.

Even the dog was restless, confined to the house because they were too scared to take her out for walks. So she did her business on the back porch. Or on the kitchen floor.

The house was in shambles. They eked by on few provisions. After the cashier at the Magic Mart refused to sell them anymore beer and cigarettes and then a scene in the Winn-Dixie with one of the Sheltons, Claude got what they needed from the PX on the fort. But only enough to last a few days. The future was too uncetain to buy in bulk.

Sometimes, Claude thought about turning himself in, just to get it over with. He even cruised past the sheriff's station one evening to see if he had the guts. Across from the brick building, he sat in his car and noticed a barred window that faced the parking lot of an office building. When he was locked up, that might be the window to his cell. He would be able to look out and watch the office workers arrive each morning. And in the late afternoon, they would leave in their cars, heading home to their wives and children. But there he'd be, day after day, a convict in stir.

But at least there would be no more waiting.

And no more Rick.

At this point, Claude and Rick were reluctant housemates, united through circumstantial evidence. But Rick had no idea what he was up against. He was scared, understandingly so, and obviously seeking reassurance from the older man, but Claude didn't have it in him to comfort anybody. He was just as lost, empty, drained of all compassion.

Just as soon take him out into the woods and plant a shovel in the back of his skull. Be doing the world a favor too. One fatal blow right between the eyes, that was all it would take. Lock me up for that crime and I'd serve my time with pleasure, Claude told himself.

This fanciful, but satisfying, solution eased the burden of waiting. But like evrything else, it was only a fantasy. His entire existence was one massive delusion, a never ending series of daydreams and nightmares. And all along, he'd been a willing participant in the machination of his demise. That it had come to this was no surprise, really. He didn't even have to wonder at the current turn of events.

He knew he had it coming. The price to pay for living in a fool's paradise.

One night Claude returned home from one of his solitary drives and found Rick seated at the kitchen table with his two BB guns and a buck knife laid out in front of him. The house was dark. Claude switched on the light, walked past without a word and picked up the bottle of Seagram's.

Rick began to speak, his voice monotone, distant.

"I'm getting kicked out of the Army. I'm losing everything I've worked so hard for. We should just leave. Take all the money we can get and go! My family will protect us. I have friends..." Rick talked as if he'd just realized the gravity of their situation. "We could hide out in the desert. Or go someplace else. Anywhere. Change our names. Create new identities. This is what I've been training for. I can make it anywhere. It doesn't matter to me. We're idiots to just wait here for them to take us. We're like... like like... rats in a cage." Rick slammed his fist on the table. "I can't go down like this. I can't!" Slumped over, he clasped at the wood and moaned, "My whole life is ruined. Everything! Ruined! I was supposed to join the Special Forces. I was gonna be a commando! I gave up all my dreams to help you and your family... I was there for you! And now... now..." Rick burst into tears. "I just can't take it anymore. I don't wanna go to jail! I don't wanna be here anymore! I just wanna go home! Why are they torturing us like this? Why can't they just get it over with already?"

As he reached a crescendo of fear induced rage, Rick whimpered and choked back a torrent of self-pity.

"I can't do this anymore, Claude. I can't..." Rick shook his head back and forth, spit and tears dripping from his chin.

Claude finished pouring a drink and started to walk out of the kitchen.

Rick lunged at him, falling to his feet and grasping the sleeve of Claude's uniform.

"You gotta help me! You can't let them put me in there! You have to make this go away!"

"There's nothing we can do!" Claude shouted.

"But this is all your fault. You cursed me! I was just trying to help you! Oh, if only I'd listened to my mother and my brothers! I never should have come with you!"

Claude slapped Rick across the face. "Snap out of it, motherfucker! It's over! So shut up and take it like a man!"

Rick crumbled onto the floor, trembling and muttering, "Why? Why? I can't..."

Claude stepped over the mush of human and walked down the hallway to his room.

He felt no pity.

He knew it was pointless.

MISTER NICE GUY

In a small conference room, I met a portly, middle-aged man. Dave, My therapist.

"In this room you are free to say whatever's on your mind," Dave told me. "You can ask questions you think are too personal to bring up in group. And if you feel the need to use expletives, that's fine too. I understand how kids talk these days. If it helps you express yourself, go for it."

Dave had an unfinished face. As I sat there listening to him talk, I imagined him with a different look. He needed something, a beard or a moustache. Maybe a goatee. Dave the beatnik. An accesory wouldn't hurt either. A pair of glasses or a monocle. That's it! A goatee and a monocle. Perhaps a tophat, like the guy on the Monopoly box. I smiled as I rearranged Dave's face.

"Do you have any questions?" he asked.

"Just when I'm getting to the second level."

"That will be determined as you participate in the program."

"But isn't my situation different?"

"Each situation is different. The important thing is to follow the rules and take advantage of what we have to offer you here."

"What about my brother? They said I'd be able to see him. But if I can't leave the ward, how can I talk to him? He doesn't like to be alone."
"Your brother will be fine. Don't worry."
I sighed and straightened my legs. "So what are we supposed to talk about then?"
"We could talk about why you're here?" Dave suggested.
"I don't know why I'm here. They didn't tell me."
"You must have some idea."
"Oh, you mean what happened with Rick, my dad and Joey?"
"Okay. Let's talk about that."
"What's to say? I found these pictures when I was snooping through my dad's stuff. They wouldn't let me smoke, so I had to take matters into my own hand. After I found them, I gave them to the social workers." I paused. "That's it. End of story."
"How did you feel about the photographs?"
"I'd rather have found some money or cigarettes, that's for sure." I laughed uncomfortably. "It sucks, you know. But what can you do?"
Dave grunted and made a note in his file.
"Anyway, I figure you guys know more about what's going on than I do," I added. "You have all the files. You've talked to my brother, right? And you've seen the photos. So... That pretty much sums it all up. With a feather in its cap."
Dave continued making notes as I blabbered on, almost against my will.
"I was just trying to do the right thing, you know? Now I'm starting to feel like I did the wrong thing."
"This program isn't about whether or not you've done something wrong."
"You lock people up as a reward?"
"We're not trying to punish you. We're trying to help you."
"Help me with what?"
"You don't feel like you have something to work on here?"
"Like what?"
"Like what happened with your father."
"Nothing happened to me, if that's what you're thinking. I'm not in any of those pictures. So... nothing to worry about there." I smiled. "I'm fine."
Dave sat there looking at me without saying a word.
"Really, I'm fine." I felt the need to repeat myself multiple times to sound convincing.
After a few minutes, Dave said, "I think we need to start getting serious." He reached into a briefcase

and placed three spiral notbooks on the table with
band names and logos scrawled into the covers.
 "Hey, my notebooks!" I'd forgotten them in the rush
to get out the door when the social workers picked us up.
 Dave spread them out on the table and flipped through the pages. "What were you trying to express in
this song, 'Fade to Black'?"
 "That's a Metallica song."
 "Yes, I see you have that written underneath. You
have an entire section devoted to what you call your
favorite rockers: 'Mommy's Little Monster,' 'Suicide's
an Alternative,' 'Annihilate This Week.' What is it
about these songs that made you want to write them
out in your notebook?"
 "I wanna be a songwriter, so I write out lyrics as
practice. I study how the verses, bridges and choruses
work together. Most of the songs in there I wrote."
 Dave flipped through the pages. "This is one of
yours: 'If telling you would kill you, to realize
would be suicide.' What did you mean by that?"
 "It just, you know, sounded cool."
 Dave turned the page. "Here you have, 'One of these
days when I have the guts I'm gonna jump right in
front of a pick-up truck.' Another one goes, 'Sometimes I just wanna blow it all away. Light a fuse and
watch the world go up in flames.' That one you titled
'Hate Bomb'."
 "They're just songs," I said with an awkward chuckle. "They aren't supposed to mean anything."
 "What kind of songwriter would you be if the songs
you wrote had no meaning?"
 "I mean, yeah, sure... they have meaning. But you're
reading them all wrong. I'm trying to come up with
songs that rock, you know?"
 "You don't think this subject matter reflects your
true feelings?"
 "No. I'm not afraid to say what I want." I laughed
to show how good-natured I was. "Look, you're totally
judging these songs based on the words alone. But
that's only part of it. My songs are about the music
as much as the lyrics. These are just words on paper,
so you have to imagine the rest of the song, how they
would be performed live--you know, once I get a band
going. It's all about the power in the music." I reachched for one of the notebooks and flipped through to
a familiar page. "Take this one right here: 'Prisoner
of Time.' This I just wrote. It starts out real mellow,
almost like a ballad, but once the verses start, it
gets fast. But not too fast. It's still building up

to the bridge. Then it's like--" I replicated the sounds of instruments with my mouth, blowing out air rapidly through parsed lips. "Dun dundun! Dun dundun! Dun dundun! Dun dundun! Then it goes back into the verses again. But after the second bridge it keeps building to the chorus where the guitars go, Chuga chuga chuga chuga. Chuga chuga chuga chuga. Then the double bass drum kicks in and it's getting faster..." I tapped my feet rapidly against the floor. "Then the lead guitar starts to wail." I pantomined the guitar parts. "Right? And then it's like, 'I'm a prisoner! Prisoner! Prisoner of time! And the walls! The walls! They're all in my mind!" I covered my mouth to mimic background vocals. "Then it goes totally insane. The drum beat is all over the place as the bass follows the lead guitar up to the crescendo: 'Prisoner! Prisoner! Break free!'" I leaned back in my chair and folded my arms across my chest. "So you see, that song's really about freedom, you know? I wasn't trying to be negative or anything."

Dave smiled at my performance. "I can see you are very enthusiastic about your music." Just when I thought we were getting somewhere and Dave would realize that I didn't need any of their help or to be a part of any program, he pushed the notebook with the plain green cover across the table. "What about this one?"

The green notebook was my journal. My mind raced as I tried to remember all the crazy stuff I'd written. I knew there were detailed descriptions of my trysts with Missy, commemorated in case I forgot anything. But I'd also written about death fantasies, the pros and cons of suicide versus running away, as well as my short autobiography, in case anybody wondered why I'd offed myself.

As Dave stared at me, I didn't know what to say. So I just sat there, trying not to look crazy.

"I think we need to start talking about why you're really here," Dave finally said.

"I don't wanna kill myself, if that's what you're thinking." I tried to be adamant but reassuring. "Honestly. I was just writing that stuff out. Half of it's bullshit anyway. Just stories I was writing. You can't hold me to that."

Dave said nothing for several minutes while I squirmed in my chair, waiting for the verdict. I could sense my diagnosis was grim. The room was hot. I was sweating bricks the longer I waited.

"Okay, our time is up for today." Dave gathered all my notebooks into a neat stack and directed me out the door.

Later that day, I met Dr. Winscott.
"I just have a few questions for you."
He clicked the end of his pen in and out as he alternated his gaze between me and my chart. "How have you been feeling?"
"Fine."
"Are you sleeping alright?"
"Sure."
"Appetite normal?"
"Yeah."
"Any recent thoughts of hurting yourself?"
"No!" I said quickly. "I never wanted to hurt myself. If you're referring to what's in my notebooks, I was just making things up, you know? Writing out loud, so to speak. I'm not suicidal." I laughed. Would somebody who wanted to kill themself laugh? I wondered.
Dr. Winscott looked up from the chart. "Any allergies?"
"Nah, I'm cool like that."

That night, Vera called me to the counter and set two small white paper cups in front of me. One had two round pills on the bottom and the other was water.
"What's this?" I asked.
"Your meds."
"But I'm not sick."
"Doctor's orders."
"What are they for?"
"Just take the pills."
I knew there was no arguing with Vera, so I dropped the pills into my mouth and chased them with the water.
"Now open wide and lift up your tongue."

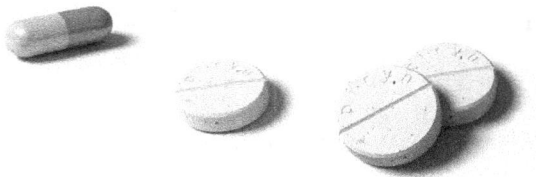

Back in the room, I told Alex, "Oh man, this sucks! I'm never gonna make it to the second level!"
"What happened?"
"They think I'm suicidal and put me on pills!"
"Bummer."
"Man, they just don't get it!"
"Yeah, well... welcome to the land of confusion, where everything is a misunderstanding."

"PRISONER OF TIME"
LYRICS BY LOUIS BAUDREY

VERSE 1

I SPEND MOST OF MY TIME WAITING
AND SO I SMOKE A LOT OF CIGARETTES
I'D SAY ABOUT A PACK AND A HALF
EACH AND EVERY DAY ~~TO START~~.

BREAK GUITAR

AND I WATCH TOO MUCH TV → BREAK
CAUSE THE LAST TIME

(2)
I WAS ANYWHERE, I WAS DREAMING

GUITAR BUILDS

SO CAUGHT UP
I WA LOOKING FOR ANYTHING
I COULD FIT IN THE PALM
OF MY HAND

TO

BRIDGE

AND SO I HELD ON TO WHAT I KNEW FOR SURE
WOULD GET ME THROUGH THE DAY.
AND LAST

THEN

THE WHOLE NIGHT LONG

— CHORUS —

DOWN TO BE DOUBLE BASS DRUM

CAUSE I'M A PRISONER!
(PRISONER) OF TIME!
AND THE WALLS!

BG

(THE WALLS) ARE ALL IN MY MIND!

(GUITAR SOLO)

VERSE 2

AND EVEN NOW IT'S STILL THE SAME
I GUESS SOMETHINGS JUST NEVER CHANGE
AND EVERY DAY I CAN FEEL MYSELF
DRIFTING FURTHER FROM THE PLAN
AND WHAT WITH ALL THESE DISTRACTIONS
AND OBSTACLES TO FALL INTO
IS IT REALLY ANY WONDER
THAT I GOT NOTHING MORE
THAN WHEN I BEGAN

BRIDGE
- AND SO I HOLD ONTO WHAT I KNOW FOR SURE
- ~~OUTED~~ WILL GET ME THROUGH THE DAY
- AND LAST THE WHOLE NIGHT LONG

→ CHORUS —
- CAUSE I'M A PRISONER
- BG (PRISONER) OF TIME
- AND THE WALLS
- BG (THE WALLS) ARE ALL IN MY MIND

MIDDLE 8:
- SOMETIMES I THINK I'VE GOT IT MADE
- BUT MOST OF THE TIME IT'S JUST A WASTE
- AND IT DOESN'T MATTER WHAT ANYBODY SAYS
- I KNOW IT'LL ALWAYS BE THIS WAY

SONG STOPS ON "OUT" (NO FADE)

THEN BACK TO CHORUS   SOLO GUITAR
    UNTIL I
    BREAK OUT BREAK OUT
    BREAK OUT BREAK OUT
    BREAK OUT BREAK OUT

From the Notebook Lyrics of Louis Baudrey

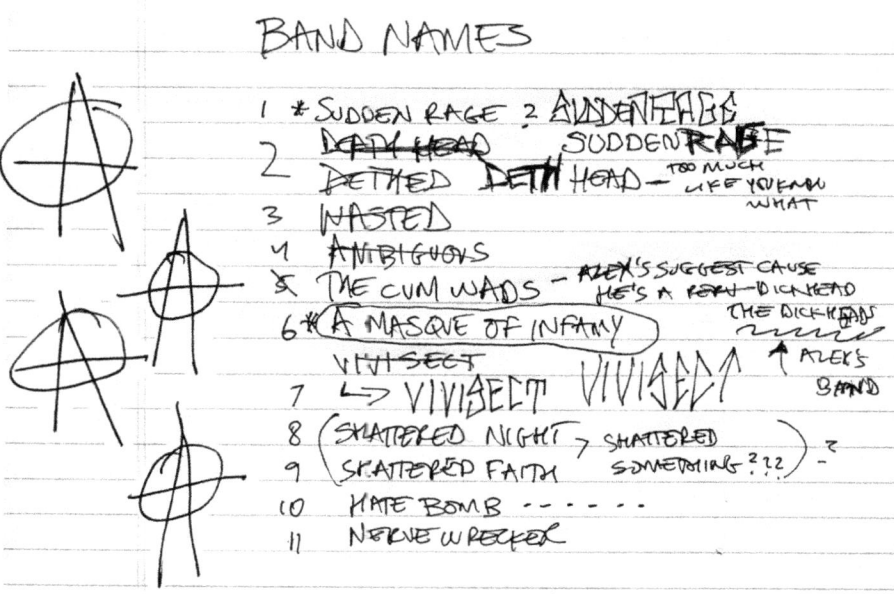

BAND NAMES

1. * SUDDEN RAGE   2. ~~SUDDEN RAGE~~ SUDDEN RAGE
2. ~~DEATH HEAD~~ ~~DETH~~ HEAD — TOO MUCH LIKE YOU KNOW WHAT
3. WASTED
4. AMBIGUOUS
5. THE CUM WADS — ALEX'S SUGGEST CAUSE HE'S A ~~FUCK~~ DICKHEAD THE DICKHEADS
6. * A MASQUE OF INFAMY
7. ↳ VIVISECT   VIVISECT   ← ALEX'S BAND
8. (SHATTERED NIGHT → SHATTERED SOMETHING???) ?
9. (SHATTERED FAITH
10. HATE BOMB - - - - - -
11. NERVE WRECKER

STATE OF ALABAMA,   *   IN THE CIRCUIT COURT FOR
           Plaintiff,   *
VS.   *   CALHOUN COUNTY, ALABAMA
                      *
▇▇▇▇▇▇▇▇▇▇▇▇▇▇ and   *   CASE NO. CC87-1070
▇▇▇▇▇▇▇▇▇▇▇▇▇▇,   CASE NO. CC87-1071
           Defendants. *

MOTION FOR CONSOLIDATION OF DEFENDANTS

    Comes now the State of Alabama by and through the Office of the District Attorney of the Seventh Judicial Circuit, pursuant to Temporary Rule 15.4(b), Alabama Rules of Criminal Procedure, to respectfully move that the defendants in the above-styled cases be joined for the purpose of trial. As grounds for its motion the State would show that the above defendants have been charged in separate indictments with offenses that could have been joined in a single indictment as the defendants are alledged to have participated in the same act or transaction or the offenses are part of a common conspiracy, scheme, or plan, or the offenses are otherwise so closely connected that it would be difficult to separate the proof of one from proof of the other.

    WHEREFORE, the State so moves and requests a hearing on ths motion to be set not less than seven days prior to trial, on this the 28th day of October, 1987.

                                                      /s/ Carolyn F. Morgan
                                                      Carolyn F. Morgan
                                                      Assistant District Attorney

CERTIFICATE OF SERVICE

    I hereby certify that I have, on this 28th day of October, 1987, served a copy of the foregoing Motion on Honorable Steve Stevens, Attorney for ▇▇▇▇▇▇▇▇▇▇▇▇▇▇, and Honorable William Broome, Attorney for ▇▇▇▇▇▇▇▇▇▇▇▇▇▇, by placing same in the U. S. mail, properly addressed and postage prepaid.

```
FILED IN OFFICE  11-5   , 19 87
R. F. (FORREST) DOBBINS, CLERK
CIRCUIT COURT, CALHOUN COUNTY.
By:_____(initials)
```

RECKONING

It was not yet dusk, but the sun had fallen behind Blue Mountain and Saks lay in its shadow. On his way home from Fort McClellan, Claude stopped at the Texaco and pumped five dollars of unleaded. As he drove down Lenlock Lane, he hit the traffic light at Saks Road. That's when he saw the squad cars in the driveway of his house.
The day had finally come.
Instantly, his mind raced with the possibility of escape. A voice screamed, This is your chance! Run! It's now or never!
Part of him wanted to keep driving past the house and get on the interstate. Go! Leave! Fuck it! Let Rick take the rap!
As tempting as the idea was, Claude immediately considered all the holes in the plan. Once he was on the lam, where would he go? And what about money? The credit union was already closed. He certainly couldn't leave behind a trail of personal checks.
There was no way to access what little money was left of his pay after he'd taken care of rent and bought groceries. There was a bag in the backseat.
He was only about twenty yards from the house. As if on auto-pilot, Claude flicked the right turn signal. He pulled into the driveway and veered to the right of the squad cars. Didn't want to block them in and then have to move his car when it was time to leave.
His muscles felt like jello as he switched off the ignition, opened the door and stepped onto the chert gravel. He picked up the bag of groceries.
Slowly, he approached the front door.
There's still a chance! the voices said. RUN!
With his hand around the door knob, Claude heard men speaking inside.
"Hello?" he said cautiously as he passed through the threshhold.
"Claude Baudrey?" A uniformed officer entered the foyer. "We have a warrant for your arrest."

"Yes, I know," Claude stammered. "Do I need to get anything? To take with me, I mean? Should I change out of my uniform?"

"You're fine as you are." The officer reached for the the bag of groceries and set it on the floor. "I have to put the cuffs on now. You understand what's going on, correct?"

"Yes, I understand." Claude turned to face the wall and held his wrists together behind his back to make it easier on the officer. He thought about the fifth of Seagrams in the bag, the cigarettes, the loaf of bread and the cold cuts... all to waste. For a moment he considered asking if he could grab the smokes.

As he listened to his miranda rights, two officers escorted Rick out of the bedroom. His cheeks were red and wet, his face twisted into a demented Halloween mask.

"This is all your fault," Rick growled.

Outside, Claude saw the Sheltons and several other neighbors watching from a distance.

"Silas!" Claude yelled. "Can you take the dog?"

Mr. Shelton nodded.

"She's a full breed," Claude told the officer as he entered the back of the squad car. "Somebody'll want her no doubt."

Much to Claude's relief, he and Rick were transported downtown in separate cars.

From this point on, he knew it was in his best interest to keep his distance from the funny looking half-Mexican/half-Japanese kid from California.

STATE OF ALABAMA,		
Plaintiff,	*	IN THE CIRCUIT COURT FOR
VS.	*	CALHOUN COUNTY, ALABAMA
▓▓▓▓▓▓▓▓▓▓ and	*	
▓▓▓▓▓▓▓▓▓▓,		CASE NO. CC87-1070
Defendants.		CASE NO. CC87-1071

MOTION FOR CONSOLIDATION OF DEFENDANTS

Comes now the State of Alabama by and through the Office of the torney of the Seventh Judicial Circuit, pursuant to Temporary Rule abama Rules of Criminal Procedure, to respectfully move that the the above-styled cases be joined for the purpose of trial. As s motion the State would show that the above defendants have been parate indictments with offenses that could have been joined in a sin nt as the defendants are alledged   participated in the same act

GRAND JURY DOCKET No. 205	**INDICTMENT** (General)	CIRCUIT COURT No. CC 87-1070

STATE OF ALABAMA
CALHOUN COUNTY

IN THE CIRCUIT COURT OF CALHOUN COUNTY, ALABAMA

OCTOBER _____, SESSION, 19 87

COUNT I (Month)

The Grand Jury of Calhoun County charge that, before the finding of this Indictment . . . . ~~████~~

whose true name is to the Grand jury otherwise unknown, did engage in deviate sexual intercourse with ~~████~~ who was less than twelve years of age, he, the said ~~████~~, being sixteen years old or older, in violation of §13A-6-63 of the Code of Alabama, against the peace and dignity of the State of Alabama.

COUNT II

The Grand Jury of Calhoun County further charge that, before the finding of this indictment, ~~████~~, whose true name is to the Grand Jury otherwise unknown, being sixteen years of age or older, did subject to sexual contact ~~████~~, who was less than twelve years of age, in violation of §13A-6-66 of the Code of Alabama,

AGAINST THE PEACE AND DIGNITY OF THE STATE OF ALABAMA

Signed _____
District Attorney, Seventh Judicial Circuit of Alabama

A TRUE BILL

Signed W. E. Dean
FORELADY-FOREMAN

Indictment received in Open Court by Judge from Foreman (Forelady) in presence of at least 11 other Grand Jurors.

Bond Set at $ 50,000

NO -or- _____, Prosecutor

Signed Harold Quattle
JUDGE

INDICTMENT FILED:
date Oct. 23, 1987

Signed: R. Forrest Dobbins   Clerk of Circuit Court
-or-
Signed: _____ Deputy Clerk - Ass't

THE STATE OF ALABAMA,   *
         Plaintiff   *
                               *
vs.   *   CRIMINAL CASE NO. CC 87-860
                               *
~~████~~,   *
         Defendant

**MOTION FOR PSYCHIATRIC EXAMINATION,
INSANITY EVALUATION AND/OR COMPETENCY EVALUATION**

FEELING BLOCKS

Joey sat at a plastic table and contemplated the lettered blocks piled up in front of him.

"Okay, children," the fat lady said. "Today, we'd like y'all to use your blocks to spell out the word you think best describes how you feel. Okay? Here is a list of words on the board, but these are only suggestions. You can use your letters to spell out any feeling you like."

Joey looked at the choices written on the chalkboard: SAD, HAPPY, ANGRY, GRATEFUL...

Each afternoon, the residents of the youth ward prison camp sat in a circle while the fat lady or one of the other gooks subjected them to word association games. Sometimes they handed out what looked like Monopoly cards, except instead of using them to advance toward a definite purpose, the cards were only to help them express their feeling. Other times, they were given crayons and asked to illustrate their feelings on construction paper. The current torture device was known as Feeling Blocks.

What's with this little kid shit? Joey always wondered. Must be some kind of trick. Like vampires after blood, the gooks were always up to something.

During their daily inquisitions, they constantly pressured him to give up the information they wanted. And even though he regarded their authority as a sham, every day their grip tightened. They'd even locked him up in a room for an entire day just becuase he asked for something to eat.

The gooks would stop at nothing to make him talk.

Twice a week, he met with a bearded man who asked about his father and Rick. And no matter how many times Joey said he had nothing to say, the bearded man kept pushing and pushing... It was always about the same thing: the polaroids. But that wasn't anything he was willing to talk about.

"I just need to talk to my brother," Joey said. Those were his orders. Louis was in charge. Not these gooks.

Joey knew they saw him as the weak one, which is why they separated him from Louis. They figured they'd get what they wanted out of him because he was a little kid. But Joey would prove them all wrong. His emotions were a currency he horded like a miser. There was nothing they could do to make him talk. He was used to torture. He knew how to take it like a man.

And if they wanted him to play with kid toys, if they somehow thought this would trick him into spilling his guts, well...

Joey smiled when he had finished arranging his feeling blocks: **FUCK THIS**

* * *

"WHERE IS MY REWARD"

Lyrics: LB Music: LB

VERSE 1
D (C G-F D) (C G-F)
WE GAVE YOU EVERYTHING — RIGHT FROM THE START
I NEVER ASKED NO QUESTIONS — WE JUST PLAYED THE PART
NOW I SEE THINGS DIFFERENT — AND I WANNA KNOW WHY
I PAID FOR THE TICKET — BUT WE DIDN'T GET TO RIDE!

CHORUS
WE GAVE YOU WHAT YOU WANTED → C F G F D
BUT YOU JUST SHUT THE DOOR → ~~C F G F D~~ TWO RUNS ONLY
WE GAVE YOU WHAT YOU WANTED → ~~C F G F D~~
SO WHERE IS ~~OF~~ MY REWARD? → C F G F D

VERSE 2
D C G F D C G F
YOU SAY I'M YOUNG — TOO YOUNG TO UNDERSTAND
BUT I DON'T HAVE TIME — TO PROVE THAT I'M A MAN
SO PUT ME ON THE STAND IN THIS TRIAL BY FIRE
IT'S ONE STEP CLOSER TO MY FUNERAL PYRE.

CHORUS X 2
REPEAT VERSE 1
CHORUS X 2
FADE

From the Notebook Lyrics of Louis Baudrey

CC- **87-1070**

TO: ALABAMA BOARD OF CORRECTIONS -- MONTGOMERY, ALABAMA -- ATTN.: CENTRAL RECORDS OFFICE.
IN RE: CONVICTION REPORT [EXCERPT-TRANSCRIPT OF OFFICIAL RECORD] OF DEFENDANT'S CONVICTION & SENTENCE.

CIRCUIT COURT — CALHOUN COUNTY — ANNISTON, ALABAMA — COUNTY SEAT.

STATE OF ALABAMA No. CC-**87-1070**
VS. ~~[redacted]~~

CHARGE: INDICTMENT [ON INFORMATION]:
I). **SODOMY 13A-6-63**
II). **SEX ABUSE 13A-6-66**

Class _____ Felony. Code Sect. _____

Judges entries at time of sentencing:
Race **-W** Sex **M-**
d.o.b. **8-18-67** age **20**

CONVICTED (crime): ~~NO CHARGE~~
COUNT ONE
SODOMY

date of orig. arrest: **8-10-** 19**87**

Class **A** Felony. Code Sect. **13A-6-66**

Youthful Offender ☐ | Habitual Offender ☐
SID NO. | AIS NO.

Judge: **Street** Pros. Atty. **C. Morgan** Def's Atty. **J. Stephens**

NOTE: In all proceedings def't in open court with or without attorney (and, if w/o then afly waived, declined, or denied on record)...
NOTE: Prior to allowing any guilty plea the court advised def't of rights and of consequences...

⊙ GUILTY PLEA : date **11-24** 19**87** plea of guilty of above stated crime. **SODOMY**
⊙ JURY TRIAL : date _____ 19___ Jury & Verdict — guilty of above stated crime.
⊙ "Y.O." CASE : date _____ 19___ ☐ guilty plea as "Y.O.". ☐ tried (by court) - guilty as "Y.O.".
⊙ SENTENCE : date **11-24** 19**87** sentenced to Alabama State Prison for term of.....
(TERM): **TWENTY (20) YEARS**
[NOTE: IF "Y.O." Case then sentence is to state custody as provided by youthful offender Act.]

⊙ CONCURRENT : [case No(s).]-
⊙ JAIL CREDIT : • date **11-24** 19**87** Jail credit ordered by court: **107 DAYS**
• date _____ 19___ Jail credit ordered by court: _____
⊙ SPLIT-SENT. : date _____ 19___ (specify):

⊙ ASSESSED : ★ Costs $ **211.00** ★ Crime Vict. Comm. $ **25.00** ★ Restitution $ _____
★ Fine $ _____ ★ Atty. Fee (re-coup) $ **800.00** ★ Removal (re-coup) $ _____
★ Other (Specify): _____

• PROBATION :
• date _____ 19___ Probation Application.
• Note: Sentence suspended [Yes—No]
• date _____ 19___ DENIED—GRANTED.
• date _____ 19___ REVOKED.
• date _____ 19___ sentence reinstated.

• APPEAL :
• date _____ 19___ Appealed.
• Note: Sentence suspended [Yes—No]
• date _____ 19___ Bonded
• date _____ 19___ Affirmed...
• date _____ 19___ Final. Cert.
• date _____ 19___ sentence reinstated.

NOTE: to best of Clerk's knowledge def't in custody.
(SEAL)

CLERK'S CERT. : State of Alabama — County of Calhoun
The foregoing is true and correct, according to the official record in stated case; -and to clerk's belief and knowledge.

DATE **11-28** 19**87**
/S/ **R.F. Dobbins**
Clerk

CC: Court File & Sheriff.

Oct 2, 1987

Judge accused of destroying porno evidence

By JOHN RONNER
Star Staff Writer

Calhoun County District Judge Larry Warren has been relieved of further juvenile cases after being accused of destroying pornographic photographs that were key evidence in a pending sex abuse case.

A complaint will be sent to the Judicial Inquiry Commission for review, and a report will be made to the attorney general's office, according to interviews with a number of persons knowledgeable about the controversy.

In the meantime, Warren continues to hear civil cases.

WHILE DECLINING to discuss specific details of the incident, Warren said Thursday he acted with good intentions and did not violate any law.

"It's unfortunate what's happened, but I don't see where I did anything improper or illegal," Warren said.

He said he was unaware that the photos would be needed in a criminal prosecution and was concerned that unauthorized persons were looking at them. He said no secure place was available in district court to protect the photographs' confidentiality.

THE CALHOUN County District Attorney's office began an investigation earlier this week into Warren's alleged burning of the photos last week. The photos had been seized by Anniston police and gathered by social workers for prosecution of the sex-abuse case. They

Judge Larry Warren

allegedly were destroyed behind the Calhoun County Family Court building on Gurnee Avenue.

"We have taken several sworn statements from the people involved, and have turned them over to Judge (Malcolm) Street," Calhoun County District Attorney Bob Field said this morning. "We have no expectation of further involvement in this matter."

Following the district attorney's investigation, presiding Circuit Judge Malcolm Street Jr. met with Warren on Wednesday, and then relieved him of his juvenile court

(Please see Judge, Page 6A)

AP Photo
in parking lot in Pasadena bricks and debris down upon vehicles

leaves of glass

California
When plates collide
Huge chunks of the earth's crust, called plates, bump and grind against one another, putting stress on earthquake faults. Along the California coast, the Pacific plate is shoving into and under the North American plate, and shifting northwest by 3 inches a year.

North American Plate

Pacific Plate

Only selected faults shown

Randolph Park unit near ready

By ROBIN DeMONIA
Star Staff Writer

The Randolph Park Community Center, which will receive final inspection Monday, should be fully operational by the end of October, according to Anniston Parks and Recreation Director Gene Cornett.

When in operation, Cornett said, the building should rival five other community centers in Anniston, and take some traffic away from the overloaded Carver Center

Judge Warren Continued from Page 1

duties. Warren continues to hear civil cases.

"An investigation into alleged improprieties, if any, is continuing, and reports are being forwarded to the appropriate body or bodies," Street confirmed Thursday. He did not elaborate.

The photographs were part of what prosecutors have called one of the worst sex cases to reach the Calhoun County Circuit Court in years.

ANNISTON POLICE and social workers had taken possession of the pornographic photos as evidence against ▓▓▓ 56, and his alleged homosexual lover.

The pair was indicted in August and charged with sex abuse and sodomy, with ▓▓▓ additionally charged with possession of child pornography.

The two were charged with raping and sodomizing a preteen male relative of ▓▓▓'s. Police said at the time of the arrests that the child has been sexually abused since he was about 5.

When ▓▓▓ and ▓▓▓ were arrested, police and social workers gathered a collection of pornographic photos showing Villar and ▓▓▓ in sex acts, officers said.

The only picture showing the boy in a sex act with one of the suspects was among the series of burned photos.

The loss of the critical photo was expected to seriously weaken the child pornography possession charge against ▓▓▓, but not necessarily the other charges.

AFTER THE ARREST of ▓▓▓ and ▓▓▓, social workers sought to take custody of the boy, and a hearing was held on the issue before Warren in district court. At that point, a portion of the pornographic photos was introduced on behalf of social workers.

From that point, the photos were in possession of Warren's court. On Tuesday, the prosecutor in the criminal case asked for release of evidence still in the custody of juvenile court. However, the photographs already had been destroyed.

Warren said he was aware of the pending criminal case when the evidence was destroyed. But he said he had understood the photos in his court's possession to be simply a small representative sample of a larger body of photos already in possession of prosecutors. He said he did not realize that the smaller batch contained key evidence.

Warren said the evidence was destroyed after his custody case was completed.

The sex abuse case against ▓▓▓ and ▓▓▓ had been scheduled for trial this week, but was postponed because of a change of attorneys for one of the defendants.

Warren was elected to the district court in fall 1986. Before that, he had worked as an assistant Calhoun County district attorney handling, among other cases, juvenile court matters.

Not so, said Biden.

"I think one of the great advantages of televised hearings is that people can make their own judgments," he said. "I think they came to the conclusion that there was no distortion, that every opportunity was accorded to Judge Bork and the White House to make his case."

...ive improvem rates" this yea

Government show a large in teenagers, his lation group wi rate. Unemplo teenagers di percent in Sep percent last m

---

HUDSON'S

SATURDAY SIZZLER
ALSO FRIDAY NIGHTS TILL 8 P.M.

Two Racks Ladies'
Designer Sportswear
One Rack 20.00
One Rack .... 1/2 Off

Junior
Coca-Cola T-Shirts
With Raised Sponge Letters
Regularly 10.00   **5.00**

Famous Stacy Adams
Men's Dress Shoes and Loafers
Regularly 44.00   **29.99**

Values to 50.00
Men's Dress Coats
Assorted Colors and Sizes   **10.00**

Large Assortment
Bath Towels
SALE   **1.97** Each

One Small Rack Ladies'
Petite Sportswear
$5, $10, $15, $20

One Rack Assorted
Ladies' Dres
Now **1/3** o
Entire Stock Coats

Junior Jea
Acid Wash Regu
Stonewashed
Union Bay • Rio • Pa

Cosmetic Sp
Ladies' Ombre Ro
Men's Pierre Cardin G
Entire Stock **1/2**

Small Selectio
Percale Sheets &
Some Discontinued
SALE **1/2** Pric

One Group
Damask Tablec
Now **1/2** Pric
60" Wide Double
Dress Fabrics Values to 3.00

CC- **87-1078**

TO: ALABAMA BOARD OF CORRECTIONS -- MONTGOMERY, ALABAMA -- ATTN: CENTRAL RECORDS OFFICE.
IN RE: CONVICTION REPORT [EXCERPT-TRANSCRIPT OF OFFICIAL RECORD] OF DEFENDANT'S CONVICTION & SENTENCE.

CIRCUIT COURT — CALHOUN COUNTY — ANNISTON, ALABAMA — COUNTY SEAT.

STATE OF ALABAMA No. CC-**87-1078**

vs.

[name redacted]

CHARGE: INDICTMENT [ON INFORMATION]:
I. SODOMY 13A-6-63
II. SEX ABUSE 13A-6-66
III. POSS. PORNOGRAPHIC MATERIAL DEPICTING MINOR 13A-12-192(b)
IV. CHILD ABUSE 26-15-3

Class **A + C**   Felony. Code Sect. ↑

CONVICTED (if dif.): **TWO COUNTS**
COUNT II SEX ABUSE   13A-6-66
COUNT III POSS. PORNOGRAPHIC MATERIAL DEPICTING MINOR 13A-12-192(b)

Class **C**   Felony. Code Sect. ↑

Judges entries at time of sentencing:
Race **W**   Sex **M**
d.o.b. **5-31-31**   age **56**
date of orig. arrest: **8-10-19 87**

Youthful Offender ☐   Habitual Offender ☐   SD/NO   A/S NO

Judge: **Street**   Pros. Atty. **C. Morgan**   Def's Atty. **Broome**

NOTE: In all proceedings def't in open court with or without attorney (and, if who they only waived, declined, or denied on record)...
NOTE: Prior to allowing any guilty plea the court advised def't of rights and of consequences

● **GUILTY PLEA**: date **11-24-19 87**   plea of guilty of above stated crime. **CT. II & III**
● **JURY TRIAL**: date_____ 19___ Jury & Verdict — guilty of above stated crime.
● **"Y.O." CASE**: date_____ 19___ ☐ guilty plea as "Y.O." ☐ tried (by court) - guilty as "Y.O."
● **SENTENCE**: _____ sentenced to Alabama State Prison for term of _____
(TERM): **10 YEARS (EA. CT.) - CONSECUTIVE (TOTAL 20 YRS.)**

● **JAIL CREDIT**: date **11-24-19** Jail credit ordered by court: **107 days**
  date _____ 19___ Jail credit ordered by court: _____
● **SPLIT-SENT.**: date_____ 19___ (specify): _____
● **ASSESSED**: ★Costs $**211.00** ★Crime Vict. Comm. **25.00** ★Restitution $ ____
  ★Fine ____ ★Atty. Fee (re-coup) $ ____ ★Removal (re-coup) $ ____
  ★Other (Specify): ____

● **PROBATION**:
  date_____ 19___ Probation Application.
  Note: Sentence suspended Yes—No   DENIED—GRANTED
  date_____ 19___
  _____ 19___ REVOKED.
  date_____ 19___ sentence reinstated.

● **APPEAL**:
  date_____ 19___ Appealed.
  Note: Sentence suspended Yes—No
  date_____ 19___ Bonded
  date_____ 19___ Affirmed...
  date_____ 19___ Final. Cert.
  date_____ 19___ sentence reinstated.

NOTE: to best of Clerk's knowledge def't in custody.
(SEAL)

CLERK'S CERT.: State of Alabama — County of Calhoun
The foregoing is true and correct, according to the official record in stated case; and to clerk's belief and knowledge.

> NO TITLE FOR THIS ONE YET
>
> ① ONE OF THESE DAYS
> WHEN I HAVE THE GUTS
> I'M GONNA JUMP RIGHT IN FRONT
> OF A PICK UP TRUCK — MAYBE "CROSSTOWN BUS"?
> BUT I NEVER HAD THAT MUCH
> NO, I'VE NEVER BEEN THAT LUCKY
> AND IT'LL TAKE MORE THAN
> A LITTLE BUMP
> TO PROVE THAT I'M
> NOT THAT TOUGH
>
> DAMN IT, I NEED A FUCKING CHORUS
> CHORD - D
>
> IT WON'T TAKE MUCH
> I JUST NEED MORE THAN A TOUCH
>
> CHORUS — ???
>
> ② I'VE SEEN THE FRONT PAGE
> NEWSFLASH AND I READ
> ALL ABOUT MY CRIMES
> BUT IF THAT'S YOU AND YOURS
> AND THEIRS, WELL, THEN
> WHERE IS MINE?
>
> ③ I WAS TIGHT ROPE WALKING
> STANDING ON SOLID GROUND
> AND WHEN THE WHISPERS
> START TO TALK
> I MOVE TO ANOTHER SIDE
> OF TOWN
> CHORUS!
>
> MUCH
> TOUCH
>
> CHORUS!!!

From the Notebook Lyrics of Louis Baudrey

Two weeks after the social workers left us at the mental hospital, they came back for Joey. Took him to a Christian group home. I got to stay at Hillcrest, where I was on the adolescent ward for 3 months. Then later, in another ward for the real whack jobs. After that I was ready for a foster home.

This picture was taken a few months after I was sent to Hillcrest. In the background are some of Alex's drawings and his Marilyn Monroe picture. They said I couldn't wear my Anarchy shirt anymore and this was what they gave me instead.

State of Alabama
Unified Judicial System

Form C44 Rev 10/86

EXPLANATION OF RIGHTS AND PLEA OF GUILT
(AFTER INDICTMENT)

Case Number

CC 87 - 1071
ID YR   Number

IN THE _Circuit_ COURT OF _Calhoun_ COUNTY
STATE OF ALABAMA VS. ~~[redacted]~~

TO THE ABOVE NAMED DEFENDANT:
This is to inform you of your rights as a defendant in this criminal case. Under the indictment returned against you in this case by the Grand Jury of this county, you are charged with the crime of _Possession Pornographic Material of Minor_ which is a Class _C_ Felony. In the event you plead guilty to said crime, or if the jury finds that you are guilty of said crime, the law provides for punishment by imprisonment in the penitentiary for not less than _1yr&1day_ or more than _10yrs_ for such offense and by imposition of a fine not to exceed $ _5,000.00_ Provided further that at a sentencing hearing should the State of Alabama prove to this Court that prior to committing this offense, you have previously been convicted of any one (1) felony, then the said imprisonment term must be for not less than _____ nor more than _____ , and a fine not to exceed $ _____ . Likewise, if the State proves you have been so convicted of any two (2) prior felonies, then the said imprisonment term must be for not less than _____ nor more than _____ and a fine not to exceed $ _____ . And, if the State proves that you have been so convicted of any three (3) prior felonies, then the said imprisonment must be for not less than _____ nor more than _____ , and a fine not to exceed $ _____ .

Further, you may be ordered to pay restitution in an amount determined by the court, for the use and benefit of the victim of your criminal offense.

In accordance with §15-23-17, Code of Alabama 1975, you shall be ordered to pay a victim compensation assessment of not less than $25.00 nor more than $10,000.

IN ENTERING A PLEA OF GUILTY IN THIS COURT, YOU ARE WAIVING A TRIAL BY JURY AND THE FOLLOWING RIGHTS TO WHICH YOU ARE ENTITLED IN THE EVENT OF A JURY TRIAL.

Under the Constitutions of the United States and of the State of Alabama you have a right or privilege not to be compelled to give evidence against yourself. In the trial of your case before the jury, you have the right to take the witness stand and to testify on your own behalf, if you so desire, but no one can require you to so testify. If you testify, you can be cross-examined by the state. If you do not testify, no one can even comment to the jury as to your failure to testify. You have the right to remain absolutely silent, but anything that you voluntarily say, with knowledge of your rights, may be used against you. Your conversations with your attorney are confidential and cannot, and will not, be disclosed by your attorney.

You have the right to stand on your plea of not guilty, and the right to a public trial before a duly selected jury. In a jury trial, the jury would determine whether you are guilty or whether you are innocent, based upon the evidence in the case.

In the trial of your case, your attorney could subpoena witnesses on your behalf, make legal objections to matters that he felt were objectionable, cross-examine the witnesses of the state, examine your own witnesses, and argue the matter before the jury. He would be bound to do everything that he could honorably and reasonably do to see that you obtain a fair and impartial trial. You have the right to have witnesses subpoenaed to testify as to pertinent facts in your favor.

In the trial of your case you would come into court clothed with a presumption that you are not guilty and this presumption of innocence will follow you throughout the course of the trial until the evidence produced by the state convinces each juror beyond a reasonable doubt of your guilt. The burden of proof is upon the State of Alabama to convince each and every juror, from the evidence in the case, that you are guilty beyond a reasonable doubt before the jury would be authorized to find you guilty. If the state does not meet such burden of proof, it will be the jury's duty to find you not guilty. You will have no burden of proof whatsoever in your trial.

To the charges set forth in the indictment you have the right to enter a plea of guilty, not guilty, not guilty by reason of insanity or any other special plea. You will enter a plea of guilty only if you are actually guilty of said crime and if you do not desire a jury trial. IF YOU PLEAD GUILTY THERE WILL BE NO JURY TRIAL, AS HAS BEEN HERETOFORE EXPLAINED TO YOU.

Your attorney will go over these rights with you, but if you have any questions about any of them, please ask the undersigned judge and he will make further explanation thereof to you.

DATE _Nov. 24, 1987_   JUDGE _[signature]_

Comes the defendant in the above-styled cause and states to the court that he has read, or has had read to him, the matters and things hereinabove set forth; that his attorney has thoroughly gone over said matters and things with him and that he, the defendant, thoroughly understands them; that he is not under the influence of any drugs, medicines or alcoholic beverages and has not been threatened or abused or offered any inducement or reward to get him to plead guilty. Defendant further states to the court that he is guilty as charged, in this case, and desires to plead guilty.

DATE _Nov. 24, 1987_   DEFENDANT ~~[redacted]~~

Comes the attorney for the above-styled defendant and certifies that the above and foregoing rights were read by the defendant in my presence, or were read to him by me, that I discussed such rights with the defendant, in detail, and that a written copy of the above rights was given to the defendant or his attorney. Having gone over his rights with the defendant, in my judgement, the defendant understands his rights.

DATE _Nov. 24, 1987_   ATTORNEY _[signature]_
Filed in Office This Date: _11 24 87_   Clerk _J.D._   By _____

COURT RECORD (White)   DEFENDANT (Canary)   ATTORNEY (Pink)

84

When I was a kid, I loved going to the Reserve Center
where my father worked so I could use one of the IBM
Selectrics. I'd type out lyrics and practice my speed
with pangrams. Sometimes I'd write stupid stories
of poems about what was going on around me, like trans-
cribing what my father or his co-workers were saying
at the time and then recite it later to get a laugh.
A few months ago, my sister showed me the following
sheet of paper she'd found with some stuff I'd typed
during the time our parents were splitting up and
when I was about to move in with my father.

Now is the time for all good men to come to the aid of their country.

Now is the time for all good men to come to the aid of their country

The quick red fox jumped over the lazy brown dog

The quick red fox umps over the lazy brown dog

Once upon a time a boy got in a fight with a big bully. The big bully
kicked the shit out of the boy. The boy went to the hospital but was not
injured too much. When the boy got out of the hospital he met the big bully
in a dark alley and kicked the shit out of him and p;ut him in the emergency
ward for ten days.

```
one day mom hit dad in the head with an ash tray
it hurt and dad didnt stay another day.
mom got mad and tryed to end her life
dad helped her and bought her a knife.
now dad lives in a apt. an the prices are low
but mom is still lives in the same shit hole.
mom gots a boyfreind who thinks i'm a punk
and dad lives like a monk.
moms boy freind is rob
and mom has not another soo.
dad drinks beer all the time
moms lips looks like she ate a lime.
mom fucks all kinds of men
when its over dad while fuck all kinds of woman.
now dad is much wiser
always suckin on a budweiser.
he has not a woory in his head
while he takes all moms bread.
there s one thing i have to say
this shit will never pay
mom has rob david and don
dad has some ljerk named john
just kidding about john
and about don
 but not about vaughn
he was stupid for stayin sc long
but some thin in his mind went dong oops that was moms voise
cause he couldent stand the noise
```

PYROMANIA
$PARE ¢HANGE
#15
MY FIRST DRUNK
(part 2 of THE ROAD AWAY FROM HOME)
Smog City
MAGAZINE
It's Better To Burn Out Than To Fade Away...
DEAFULA
3$
#4
Sep. 2010
Proof I Exist #12
"Week One"
Les Carnets de Rastapopoulos
"Osem"
8
INSIDE:
Always Already
THE LA-LA THEORY
#6
OBSOLETE! #7
SciFi DIY ISSUE
CHEER THE EFF UP.
The Zines I Read
BRAINSCAN 21
irreconcilable differences
#6
SHARDS OF GLASS IN YOUR EYE!
Endorsed by doctors at Harvard!
Supplement Facts
FREE
100%
Collated Zine
28 pg
Helps Promote Comedic Health
Since 1995
I Wanna Believe
Conspiracies & Shit
BEFORE THE WORLD ENDS ... (AGAIN)!!!
XEROGRAPHY DEBT
READ THE STARTLING REVELATIONS!
WORLD BURNS WHILE INSIPID MEMES DISTRACT THE MASSES!
SMALL PRESS NEXT ON TERROR WATCHLISTS
GET READY TO DIE FOR YOUR ART!

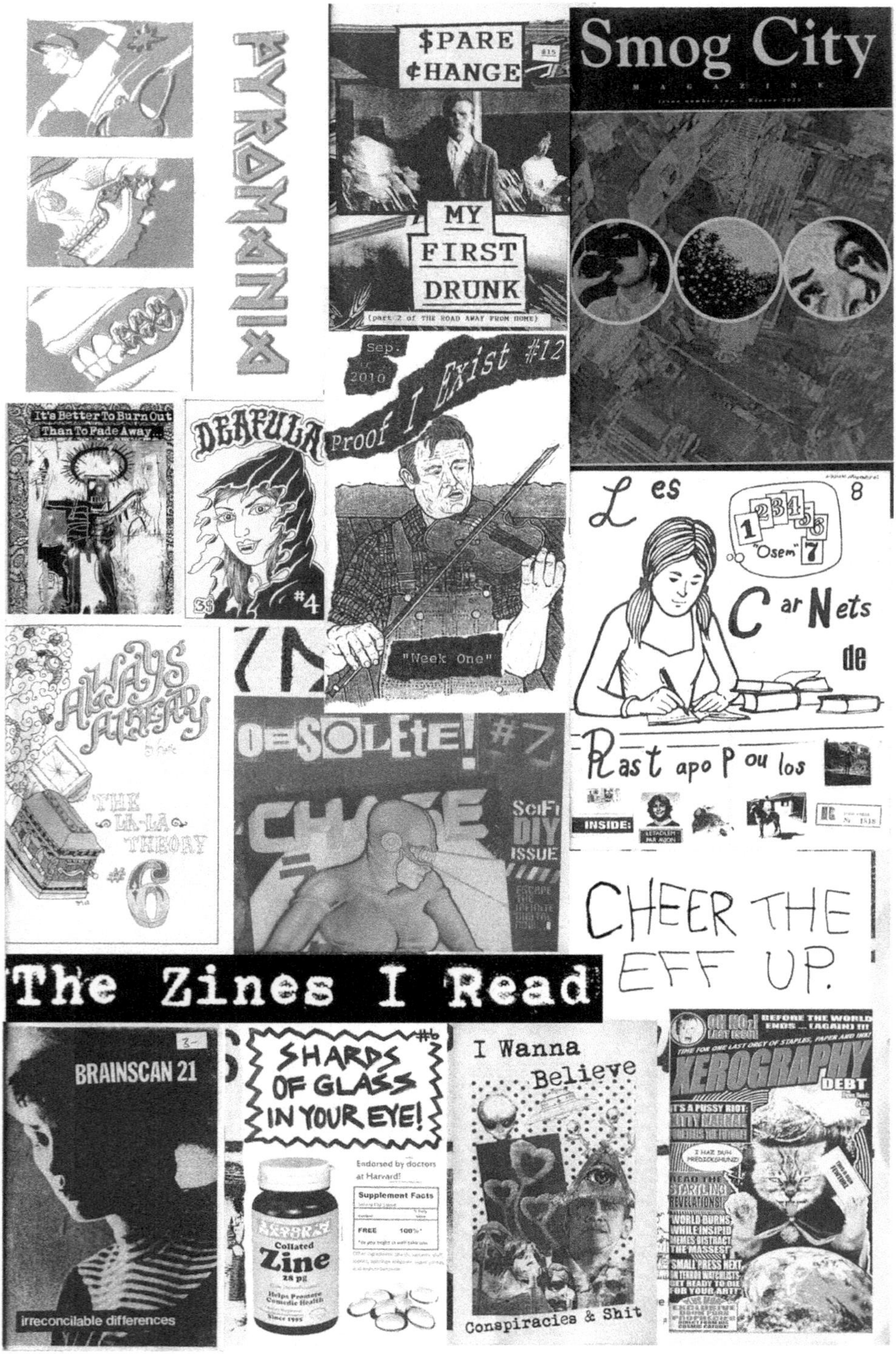

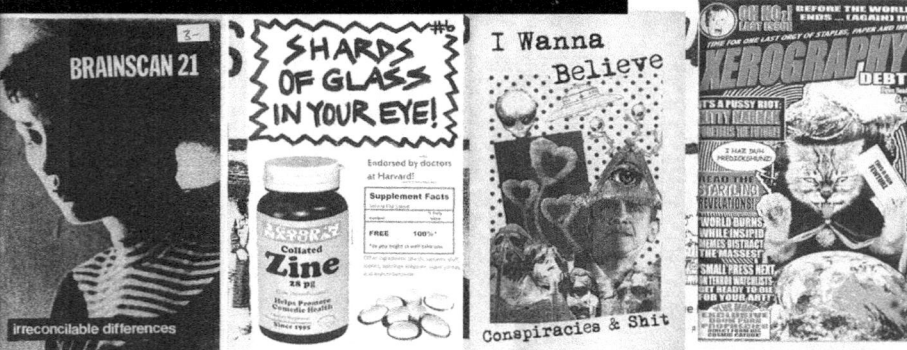

I connected with Katie, who creates the zine **The La-La Theory**, on tumblr, a site I tend to waste more time on than I should. After discovering that we shared a lot of the same interests, we set up a trade. She sent me **The La-La Theory #6: Always Already**. **The La-La Theory** is a zine about language. Katie writes in the preface, "I'm not all that impressed with humanity. But I'll keep clinging to words, language, communication, connection, writing, poetry, books, conversation, like it's a lifeline. BECAUSE IT IS." Well, any zine that starts off with a bold statement like that has me quickly turning the page to read more. **The La-La Theory #6** is a hodge-podge of material, including three sets of etymologies, detailed "reviews" of several old language textbooks she discovered in thrift stores (her analysis of these books is way more entertaining than it would seem from any brief description this review can afford, but trust me, Katie knows how to have fun with random critique), there's also a piece on found poetry and an interview with an adapter of novels into manga books. The main feature of this issue, and where the subtitle "Always Already" comes from, is an article on a Portuguese word that doesn't have a counterpart in English: Saudade, loosely translated to "a sense of longing for something that is lost and probably can't be found again." Through her research, Katie finds two foreign words with similar meanings, one in Finnish: kaiho, and another in Welsh: hiraeth. Trying to understand how one can experience the sentiment behind these words as an English speaker but to have no native word to express it leads Katie down a linguistic path that includes the literal translation of an Einstruzende Neubauten lyric: "Always already." From there, she ponders the powerful way language and culture intersect. And then there is a very nice poem she'd written about her original discovery of the word kaiho. I'm not sure if my description has done this zine justice, but I absolutely love zines that challenge me intellectually and get me thinking about things I hadn't thought of before. If you feel the same way, you will no doubt like **The La-La Theory** as well.

Katie included a few other zines, including a series
of stories she inhereted from her family called "This
was before you were born" and one called Man Is The
Hero of Geography, about an old geography textbook
she picked up at a yard sale. A few pages had been
filled in somewhat randomly, but enthusiastically, by
a sixth-grader, and in the spirit of his responses,
Katie has filled in several pages with her own random
and enthusiastic responses and printed them up for
our pleasure. Contact: PO Box 284, Jenkintown, PA 19046

Deafula #4 is about work, from the perspective of
a deaf woman. I reviewed issues 1 through 3 in Piltdownlad #5 and my esteem remains the same: **Deafula**
is a great zine, and in my opinion, an essential zine.
It's cool to see copies in several distros and I recommend getting them before they go out of print. I'm
lucky to have most, from number one to this latest
issue, including 3.5, her contribution to the 24 Hour
Zine Thing, about losing her religion. Two things I'd
like to say about **Deafula** this time around: I really
dig her layouts, and what I like best isn't just the
insight into what it's like to be deaf in America, it's
Kerri's writing and her style, her take on life, which
just so happens to be on mute some of the time.
Contact: PO Box 18013, Philadelphia, PA 19147.
(New Address)

Shards of Glass in Your Eye! is a fun perzine that
doesn't take itself too seriously. And there's nothing wrong with that! Kari has sent me several issues
so far and I've found them quite charming. As a fellow
LA resident, I've met so many people who have moved
here and share her fascination with celebrity and the
infinite sprawl, especially coming from a remote place
like Michigan's Upper Peninsula, like Kari. As an LA
native, it's easy to be jaded to the splendor of movies
and TV, having grown up in the shadow of Hollywood.
But we all have our stories of brushes with fame. It's
hard to escape. Just don't talk about it to your
friends who live in the middle of nowhere or they'll
think you're an asshole. So it's a fine line. Fortunately, only part of each issue of **Shards of Glass...**
deals with celebrity sightings. The rest is about Kari's
life, her experiences, her impressions of the world
around her, sprinkled with various tidbits of varying
comedic value. Write to Kari Tervo: PO Box 7831,
Beverly Hills, CA 90212.

EDDIE RUSSELL ZINE

One of the cooler zines I acquired at the Portland Zine Symposium was Marc Parker's **Breakfast for Dinner**. It was great chatting with Marc, somebody I remembered from the alt.zines days. Despite knowing his activities on that newsgroup as Zine Thug, I hadn't read any of his zines before, so I was happy to check out the first issue of **Breakfast for Dinner**. A mixture of simple cartoons and typewritten text give this zine an appealing aesthetic. The stories were heartfelt and obsorbing. One of the first zines I read when I got home from Portland. Contact: mrparker@zinethug.com.

I also picked up a few comics by John Isaacson at the Portland Zine Symposium. One called **Ride The Lightning**, based on the lyrics from the Metallica album, was a must-have. Anybody who's still nostalgic for the time when Metallica were a viable force in thrash metal will really get a kick out of this comic, with most of the lyrics depicted in John's skilled artwork. Another comic of his that I couldn't resist was **Pyromania #3**, which includes stories about getting into a fight with his friend, buying his first Def Leppard tape, worrying about being a poseur and becoming metal. This type of storytelling is my favorite and the kind I practice (albeit not through illustrations), so I'm predisposed to like John's comics. Since the Zine Symposium, he has sent me a couple copies of his review zine **Feedback**, wherein he reviews shows in comics and reviews albums and zines in the back in type. John also wrote the **Do-It-Yourself Screenprinting** book. His website is unlay.com

I've recieved a couple issues of the **Eddie Russell Zine**. The first one came with a small collection of trinkets and stickers as well as a letter opener that has since entered into heavy rotation in my house. I use it not just to open letters, but also packages, bags of chips and as a mini paper slicer. The last issue came with a handmade badge made from a bottle cap. The zine itself is full of photocpied images and visual shenanigans, with short interviews with bands and record reviews. There some deft ingenuity to this **Eddie Russell** enterprise and I hope it continues to germinate, and show up in my mailbox. Contact: paperdolldistro@gmail.com

   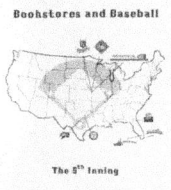

I'm always glad to be on Ken Bausert's mailing list
and recieve the latest issue of **The Ken Chronicles**.
Ken writes about his life as a senior citizen, but
there is very little about his writing and observ-
ations that I typically identify with somebody over
65. The best issues, for me, are the ones that deal
with his travels. Ken is hardly an idle spectator
in the world, so when I read about his recent trip to
Europe, I wasn't surprised that it didn't mirror the
tales I've heard from other people in his age group
who've ventured across the pon. While I was in New
Orleans during my period of exile, I spent a good
amount of time at a coffeehouse in the Garden District
that had the strongest wifi connection and
decent coffee. (New Orleans is seriously lacking in
good coffee--all blends, usually flavored, and no sin-
gle origin, but that's another story...) One day,
I was sitting outside when a young woman and a group
of older folks took the table next to mine. Based on
what I easily overheard, the woman lived in the neighborhood and the older people were relatives visiting
from out of town. They had just come back from Europe.
As I listened to them talk about their trip, I found
it hard to believe that Europe could sound so boring.
I mean, they might as well have been reading from a
travel brochure. At the time, I was talking regularly
to an old friend who currently lives in Berlin. My
neighbors were from France. So I was getting an ear-
ful on Europe and the various customs and numerous
differences with the US. Well, when Ken went to Europe,
he wasn't content to stick to the typical American
abroad experience. Since I've read a lot of his zines,
I knew Ken would be just as curious as I am about
the infamous spas in Germany. I figured that he'd
want to check them out, and I was really impressed that
he went au natural, as is the custom. Since I'd been
having a conversation about German spas and beaches,
where clothes are less than optional, I thought it
was very cool that he was willing to participate in
a very non-tourist way. I'm still not sure what I
would do in the same situation. Contact Ken Bausert:
2140 Erma Dr., East Meadow, NY 11554

At the end of **Ladybeard,** the title of which is self-explanatory, the author writes, "Anyone who is ok with me being me is ok by me." I thought this was a really cool way to end this very short, but very personal zine about self-discovery and self-acceptance. Highly recommended to those interested in body-acceptance and gender roles. Contact: beardedladyzine@gmail.com

The latest issue of **Bookstores and Baseball** covers new territory, new bookstores, new book fairs and new baseball parks. To me, this zine is about family. I've reviewed past issues and that is always my takeaway. Which is so inspiring, to think that a family can merge all their interests into a road trip and not have it end in a dysfunctional trip to hell and back. (And I don't imagine I'm just channeling my own experiences with that family dynamic.) No, the LaBountys make it look easy. That I'm also fascinated by bookstores and book fairs makes me a big fan of this zine from Blue Cubicle Press. Contact: PO Box 250382, Plano, TX 75025

I read Both by Accident and Design, Both by Chance and Circumstance and Knowledge and Naivete one after another, so they are forever ingrained in my mind as a whole. The anonymous narrator behind these three zines seems to write just as she lives her life: without a filter. Things can get awkward around her. Fast. As I started reading the first zine, I was drawn into the world of a woman in Melbourne trying to find meaningful work in the corporate setting, or at least something not completely soul-crushing, and, for the most part, failing. She quits jobs. She is fired from jobs. She is often disturbed by what her employers ask her to do, and yet she tries to do the best she can, happy to have the work. She refers to her misadventures in these offices and storefront as zine fodder. Her struggle to stay employed, so common among creative types, is entertaining, and not just due to its inherent schadenfreude. The writing is candid and friendly. There is a compelling vibrancy to the narrative that propels me forward. The most absorbing event in these three zine, at least to me, was the story of how she was giving private English lessons to a Persian man, sessions that took place at all hours of the day, and eventually began to seem like dates, given their circumstances and timeframes. And even though she was convinced that the guy was gay, she enjoyed her position as educator and confident, until one day things got weird... and, then, well... It all became another zine story.
Contact: GPO Box 4201, Melbourne, Victoria 3001,
Australia.

Two Nights in Canberra and Other Things I Would Usually Say No To is a zine about Elle's two day road trip to attend the Canberra Zine Fair. After learning some interesting facts about Australia (the capital is in a backwards pre-fab non-city, there are rabbits everywhere and very few kangaroos), I enjoyed the play by play as a series of misadventures ensue. Part of me was thinking, Does crazy shit just follow Elle around, despite her alleged attempts to avoid them? There are hassles with the van, fellow travelers abandoning the trip at the last

A DISORDERLY ZINE about a zine fair in Canberra as told by participants from the west and east coast. AND one of the organisers. invl involving some disorderly travel 2013

moment, vague directions to the house where they are staying, and a bewildering layout of a city very few companions have ever even visited. Then there are mix-ups at the house, where to sleep, a pissed off French-man and a murder story. And that's all before they even make it to the fair. When I finished reading this zine, I really wanted to know how the folks she'd written about felt when or if they read it. I was impressed by how candidly Elle described her experiences/perceptions at the zine fest and among her companions. In her international mailer, she included a small cache of treasures as well as a microzine about the fest from the other participants. And the genial impressions recorded in this small affair seem to mirror most typical reports from all zine fairs: polite and to the point. Nothing along the lines of what Elle had depicted. This isn't to suggest that the Canberra Zine Fair was rife with disaster and chaos, or anything like that. But, it was a joint effort to produce a public event with normal human interactions, which at times can be awkward, weird, unpleasant, upsetting, creepy, infuriating and a million other emotions all wrapped up in one. I think this zine is a brave document of what most zine fests are really like. And a testament to human behavior, which zinesters are not immune to just because they participate in a DIY, culturally-aware activity.
Get in touch with Elle: GPO Box 4201, Melbourne, Victoria 3001, Australia.

Les Carnets de Rastapopoulos

Les Carnets de Rastapopoulos is a zine from Canada about the author's numerous pen pals during the 80s. Issue 8 dealt with his attempt, as a kid, to find a pen pal behind the Iron Curtain. In number 9, he tries to reconnect with some of his pen pals 25 years later. I find this zine intriguing. Growing up long before the internet and even cheap long distance calls, writing letters was more than a pastime. It was a vital form of communication. I had some pen pals when I was in elementary school, mostly in Vermont, a state I was obsessed with at the time, being a geography nerd. As I got older, I went the way of the bad seeds. But I was always interested in maps and other cultures. I was especially fascinated by Eastern Europe. I guess there was just a certain type of kid who grew up during the height of the Cold War and was drawn to the mystery of life behind the Wall. Through the news, political gesturing, TV and movies, we were inundated with this sense of the East being a prison state full of god-hating commies who wanted nothing better than to destroy our way of life and start a nuclear war. For whatever reason, I didn't buy into this belief. I saw the East as an exotic place, full of dark-eyed girls with stories to tell in thick foreign accents. During my travels, staying in youth hostels and then, later, selling books at a flea market in West Hollywood, where a large population of Russian emigres live, whenever I met somebody from the former USSR, I asked as many questions as I felt the person was willing to answer. I learned a lot about life in the Eastern Bloc this way, particularly how vast the misconceptions we had of them actually were. Despite my interest in the USSR, it is only by coincidence that I married a girl from Ukraine. I wasn't THAT obsessed... I mean, it's not like I ever learned to speak Russian. My wife, even though she left the "old country" when she was 13, does not come off as foreign.

A cool thing about living with somebody who grew up behind the Iron Curtain is all the access to personal experiences of life in the Soviet Union. During the seventies, it wasn't that bad, relatively speaking. Sure, you couldn't own a car unless you were a party member and clothes and other things most Westerners saw as basic amenities, were considered luxury items.

So to get new threads, you had to save extra money from your meager paychecks for months and months. In the eighties, because of glasnost, most kids had access to pop culture through TV and radio (the Iron Curtain couldn't repel electromagnetic waves). Some of the most interesting post-punk music I've heard comes from places like Yugoslavia and Russia. I think there is something more emotionally significant to finding a punk record in a place like Belgrade or Moscow than in London or New York. Especially when they were forced to bury their albums in the ground so they weren't confiscated by the authorities. Kids in the Eastern Bloc fetishized Western goods, most of which we took for granted. My wife loves to tell the story of how it took a year of pleading and begging for a Barbie doll until her parents were able to get one smuggled into the country for a hundred dollars through some associate of a friend who know somebody who knew somebody... (Of course, within a week of finally getting the doll, she cut its hair off.)

   The way my in-laws talk, despite the lack of luxury goods and brand names and jeans and other "entrapments" of capitalism, they lived a peaceful life that revolved around work and family. They couldn't travel freely, but they had a dacha on the Black Sea for a month each year. After the Soviet Union collapsed, however, everything changed. The country was thrown into chaos and my wife and her family were lucky, they already had family in the states and were able to emigrate easily through the Jackson-Vanik Amendment.

   So what does any of that have to do with **Les Carnets de Papadoupalous**? Probably not much, but maybe some similar cultural exchanges took place between the author of this zine and his many pen pals. I hope so, anyway. Write to: 2-7 Larch St., Ottawa, ON K1R 6W4 Canada.

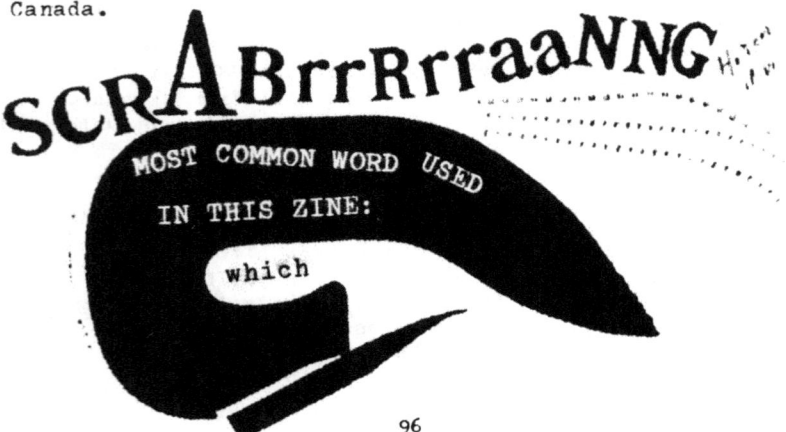

Due to the chaotic and uncertain nature of my recent move to New Orleans, many of the zines I picked up in Portland and San Francisco, along with many that were mailed to me in trade, were donated to Skylight Books, who used them in grabbags and over giveaways during the evenful week of the LA Zine Fest, which seemed a fitting way to lighten my load. I hope they all fell into appreciative hands. Some that I enjoyed but don't have the space to comment upon: Brainscan, Burn Collector, Cheer The Eff Up, Doris, Dear Shane I tried to Kill Myself, I Wanna Believe and the very intriguing Conspira/torial. There are so many great zines out there and so many that don't get the recognition they deserve.

NAME.................... CLASS.................. DATE..................

from Man Is The Hero of Geography

chapter 11
THE LOW COUNTRIES:
A MAN-MADE LANDSCAPE (pages 91-98)

A. GETTING ACQUAINTED WITH THE LOW COUNTRIES

DIRECTIONS: Using the map in your textbook, answer the following questions:

1. Name the Low Countries: *sleep paralysis*
2. What country is south of the Low Countries? *migraine*
3. What country is east of the Low Countries? *déja vu*
4. What sea forms the western boundary of the Low Countries? *night terrors*
5. The elevation of most of the Low Countries is *exploding head syndrome*
6. The most important river in these countries is the *Anxiety* and it runs through *Depression*
7. Antwerp is located near the mouth of the *Tinnitus* river.

F. OBSTACLES—NATURAL AND MAN MADE

1. DIRECTIONS: In the space provided below, write a brief report showing how natural features such as mountains and deserts have served to hamper the development of the Middle East and North Africa.

Stuttering and stammering are the same thing. A big enough leap in logic turns two sentences into a poem. Don't make a pest of yourself. Keep your head about you. Don't talk like that to your mother. Don't talk like that.

APPENDIX

1. I really wanted to call the book Sucks, Alabama--
a much catchier title, for sure. But I felt like
people would perceive the book as a slam on the state
of Alabama, which it most definitely is not. While
my teenage self wouldn't have flinched at possibly
alienating readers, I've grown somewhat squeamish
in my old age.
2. I would like to point out here that a lot of work
goes into putting this zine together, especially with
all the typing. For no other reason, this is why I
mention that it's written on an Olympia manual. I see
many typewriter fonts in zines these days and I often
wonder what kind of machine they're using (or if
they're faking with computer generated font). I have
no real judgement either way. I'm just curious.
On a side note: see letters section for more comments
on the use of typewriters.
3. Although the other parts are in third person, I
kept mine in first person, for no other reason than
it was easier to use the text that matched the published version, but there are slight variations and
additional bits. This is no compensation if you've
read the book (BTW, I do trades on the book too),
so for that, I apologize.
4. Fortunately, I was able to send away for the court
records, though it took a while for the clerks to find
the files in the storage warehouse where they'd been
kept since 1987. I even lucked out and didn't have to
pay the copy charge because of how long it took.
Getting the newspaper articles was a much more comp-
licated ordeal. They were only available on microfilm
at the local university. So my wife and I ended up
spending a long afternoon fighting with students who
had slacked on writing research papers to gain access
to the microfilm readers and scan through each day,
from June through September, of the Anniston Star.
5. Namely, my little brother.
6. There have been threats.
7. Even though it's not.
8. Only because I use dialogue and a narrative
structure.
9. I guess in the end I kind of did write a memoir,
but it's still labeled a novel on the cover. For
more information on how memoirs have caused immeasur-
able problems for authors, remember A Million Little
Pieces? Also, look up the scandals that surround
other landmark titles in that genre: Running with
Scissors, A Heartbreaking Work of Staggering Genius,

Stephen Elliott's books... The way I look at it, what does it matter what you call it if it's about getting the story out of your system. It's no skin off my nose if readers think it's made up, or only partially true. I told the story I needed to tell.

10. If you really are curious, google the name Eric Jeffrey Villar. My father's first name is Vaughn.

11. Incidentally, The Nasty Oh-Dear is the prologue to the novel and, once the current printing is gone, will go out of print. For obvious reasons. Before I put out The Nasty Oh-Dear, I hadn't published anything from the novel. Putting that story out (which was one of the first things I wrote on the subject) was a very emotional excercise in finally releasing part of this work to the public. I was very tortured about it and even tore up my first mock-up in a fit of angst and self-loathing. It was such a personal story, one I'd always kept hidden from everyone, friends as well as myself. I always wrote about stupid shit like girls, getting fucked up and running around. So it was a bold move for me to put it out as a zine. And what better format? I'm glad that I did it. But now that it's part of a novel--a larger work-- I don't want it to seem like a promo thing. Nor do I want this zine misinterpretted as some kind of vehicle or a thinly veiled advertisement. With "Institutionalized," I am completed a story I couldn't finish in the confines of the novel. But if it still comes across as promotional, I apologize. You can stop reading now. Seriously, there are a ton better zines out there. May I reccomend a few? Please see the section titled "The Zines I Read."

(c) 2013 Kelly Dessaint

Second Printing 2014

Artwork on page 19 by Walt Hall
Artwork on pages 49, 64 & 67 by Irina Dessaint

Thanks to all the folks who have read and commented on past issues of this zine, and to those who have shared their own zines. The focus of Piltdownlad is communication, making connections and sharing stories. To that end, I welcome all trades and/or letters of comment. Special thanks to Eloise.

ISBN: 1-930935-37-4

PILTDOWNLAD

A PERSONAL NARRATIVE ZINE

AVAILABLE TITLES

Piltdownlad #7: THE MURKY REALM - A biographical sketch of an improbable union... the story of how my folks got together, fell apart, came back together just to fall apart again. "...meticulously crafted and thoroughly fascinating..." - One Minute Zine Reviews 44pp./5.5"x7"/ $3.00

Piltdownlad #8.5: THE CULT OF TEDDY RUXPIN - How I lost religion, discovered punk and made true friends after moving to small town Alabama. 40pp./4.25"x5.5" $2.00

Piltdownlad #9: PAMPHLETERIA: The Rise and Fall of Phony Lid - Adventures in the publishing underground. The first of a proposed three part series on how I started a publishing company in the kitchen of the only house in an Alabama trailer park. 64pp./5.5"x8.5" perfect bound $5.00

THE OLYMPIC SPIRIT AND OTHER STORIES - Three zines in one book. Collects volumes 1 and 2 of the Guero Chingon Stories along with Junior Careers: Adventures of a Teenage Candy Salesman. Tales of growing up in LA's San Gabriel Valley. 120pp./5.5"x8.5" $7.00

A MASQUE OF INFAMY - My autobiographical novel about moving from LA to small town Alabama in the 80s, discovering punk rock, rebelling against the rednecks and bible-thumpers, dealing with an abusive home life and ending up in a mental hospital. "... twists the horror of growing up in a highly dysfunctional family into a hilarious tale of survival." --Lydia Lunch 320pp./5"x8" $14.00

All prices postpaid in US.

To order, send cash, money order or trade to:
Kelly Dessaint, Po Box 22974, Oakland, CA 94609
Order online through kellydessaint.com.

KEEP PRINT ALIVE!

www.ingramcontent.com/pod-product-compliance
Lightning Source LLC
Chambersburg PA
CBHW061336040426
42444CB00011B/2944